RECENT EVENTS

POEMS: 1994

KEVIN MAGEE

HYPOBOLOLEMAIOI

SAN FRANCISCO 1995

let them that are broken go free
and tear asunder every unjust writing

Ambrose, *De Nabuthae*

Some of these poems first appeared
in the pages of *Chain, lyric &, Mirage #4*
(Periodical) and the *festschrift* for Robin Blaser
from *The Capilano Review* (Vancouver)

Cover graphics by Richard Zybert
with special thanks to Kim Farmer
and Leo Tannenbaum, editor of
Out of the Jungle

Made in an edition of 500 equal copies
in San Francisco, California
and Ann Arbor, Michigan

ISBN: 0-9649595-0-X

NORMA COLE / KEVIN KILLIAN
THIS WAY TO ADVENTURE

The world is screaming: let those screams be heard throughout the land! The voices of the disenfranchised and deracinated speak everywhere in the pages of Kevin Magee's new book *Recent Events*.

It's a jumbo book steeped in many sources, as Magee's "indissoluble sympathy" extends in all directions, to the work of his contemporaries (Susan Howe, Bertolt Brecht, Mary Engle, Charles Bernstein) and to figures from a past distant as the future to most of us - Shakespeare; Mary Shelley; Chaucer, Langland, Karl Marx. He situates himself among these great names in order to bring forward the noise and the worth of the unheard - "triumphant appropriator!"

The writing is sometimes a direct call to action, stimulated, abrupt, final; and in other sections a dreamy, meditative tone takes over the "story." In his multiple address, Magee recuperates the fractured lineage of poetic engagement with issues of hunger, labor, and love. This book asks the question, how do we hope for solidarity in the face of the dissolution of the unified self - as an *idea*. As recent events approach the apocalyptics of *Blade Runner*, we hear the "off-world" screaming too.

Like Robert Duncan's *Bending the Bow*, *Recent Events* is a book of atropaic magic. It uses charms, spells, the rhythms of nursery rhyme and folk fairy tale to ward off the evil that hovers around us. Ritual, repetition, the sheer bigness of this project are all articulated to explode the aporia of current political hegemony. Charles Olson might have been predicting the Kevin Magee phenomenon when he wrote, to Robin Blaser [1957]: "Hold fast to yr power over old form, let you only be busted out of it like the door of a safe when some nitroglycerin you may not even know has been applied to the crack in yr door, blows you open..." Kevin Magee is the Jimmy Valentine *de nos jours*.

RECENT EVENTS IS A DOCUMENTARY WORK

Both in Nancy Shaw's letter to Kevin Killian reprinted in *Writing from the New Coast: Technique* and in the transcript of the Kootenay intervention at the 1993 New Coast Conference in Buffalo, reprinted in the first issue of *Chain* magazine, the phrase "reactionary expressionism" appears alone, singly and singled out, without its country cousin: "revolutionary expressionism."

Expressionism was (before the political context vanished in an ocean of real blood) the ground of dialectical thinking for Brecht, Benjamin, Lukács and Bloch.

The historical determinants of Expressionism are to be found in the social trauma of World War.

It may well be that every tendency of what the Academy calls Modernism was driven underground by the long range guns of the Second (or Middle) World War.

On October 11, 1993, in Oakland at the Mills College panel, *The Poet and the World of Her Influence*, Susan Howe impatiently—almost bitterly—declared: "I'm sorry. Poetry is Revolutionary."

Since the end of what Charles Bernstein, in *A POETICS*, calls the Second War (he says the effects of it are still largely repressed, that we are just now beginning to come out of the shock), all we have had is the reactionary form of Expressionism, or Academicism, that took hold in the Workshop System in the United States after the Second War—unattached to and unattacked by its mortal enemy and polar demon.

Bernstein says we are just beginning to remember the Second War, or is it that we are just now beginning to anticipate the Third?

WRITING IS MY VITAL HABIT
Emily Greenley

When I write, I am "expressing" something: writing is the formulation of an internal (emotional, intellectual) process which by its intensity or originality demands to be given form.

Good writing, further is the *making of an expression* that transforms the feeling or thought beyond mere transcription.

To "express oneself" and to "make an expression" are of course not disconnected activities. The second, however, to the extent to which a new or singular statement is constituted, is always operative in good writing.

When I started writing at age 15 I used the form (in this case, poetry) to say what I felt: both components, the *generative* (what I call the "process which demands to be given form") and the *generated* (the verbal overlay, or *expression*) were active and interacting. But because I was inexperienced, the work distorted the underlying impulse by a rococco language.

The pressure of criticism from outside and changes in the writer produced a new writing, one which I think has reached relative maturity in the last few years. My writing does, in the act of it, perform a cathartic function. Sometimes it must be the only means by which I can exorcise, or repress, anxiety or despair.

With the poem in my hands I have proof that I can *make* something: the words I have set down are apt to carry unintended meanings that, in combination, illuminate or complicate the original message. For a finished poem is anything but bare statement: it is a complex of sound and sense, an "expression" which, like a facial expression, can be projected and received in many ways while retaining an essential identity.

Freud says that the artist is "originally ... (one) who turns from reality." Rejection of reality, whether chosen by or forced on one, means insanity. Freud sees the restoration of the artist in others' acceptance of his work as an alternate construction of reality. What this means, I think, is that the artist's success derives from a simultaneous rejection of reality and insanity. It is true at least for me that writing is a conscious and calculated activity, one which is impossible when I am truly distressed.

"Past distress," though, is usually my theme: no matter how recent or continuing the trouble, I am able to construe it as resolved in the saying of it.

[Note: This statement accompanied ten poems Emily Greenley submitted in her senior year at Harvard for the Rona Jaffe/Radcliffe College Prize in Creative Writing. She did not get the prize. On her copy of the title page she wrote "lost this one!" and at the end of her statement after this sentence, "The prize money would help me tremendously through a crucial and financially insecure time," she wrote "Oh well!" I have taken the title from the part of the statement not reprinted here. I taught Emily Greenley during her freshman year at Harvard and since October 1990 when she took her life I have been, without formal designation, her literary executor. William Corbett.]

from WRITING FROM THE NEW COAST: TECHNIQUE

We will never know what transformations Emily Greenley might have brought to the immanent return of delirium and nightmare, history and apocalypse, tracings of which may be found in the thwarted works of—among others—Hart Crane, Jack Spicer, Sylvia Plath and Danielle Collobert, all of whom self-destructed in the absence of a fluid and elastic polysexual/polylingual, feminist/[marxist] culture.

A pair of Greenley's couplets:

> The unbelievably pretty ladies
> had a good bit of luck

> That were born with a body
> that would accomodate fucks;

[Note: The semi-colon at the end of the rhyme weirdly replicates the semi-colon Paul Engle inserts into the sentence he writes to his 17 year-old daughter containing the news that her mother is drinking a bottle of gin a day].

In Emily's rhyme I hear the rage of a young poet who was preparing to fight her way out of the prison camp called the University Writing Workshop where, despite the desperate efforts of a small number of isolated and harrassed poets employed there, young poets are routinely processed, mutilated and killed in the competitive arena of prizes and awards, commercial publication, the false allure of professional identity, and the lie that there will be teaching jobs.

My first job when I went to study poetry at the University of Iowa in 1981 was organizing the papers of Paul Engle, the so-called father and certainly the founder of the Iowa Writers Workshop.

Having no training as an archivist, I wound up doing more reading than collating and found, buried among letters from Robert Lowell demanding more money and Allen Tate attaching a page of interminable, tight-fisted stanzas along with other business matters, some two hundred pages of letters written over three months from Mary Engle to her daughter Mary who was 'finishing' at Spence in Brooklyn before going on to Radcliffe.

The letters begin in the middle of the last big snow in the first week of March, 1959, and end in the tumult surrounding her daughter's graduation, an event which against the daughter's wishes mushroomed into a society affair hosted by Adelaide Marquand, the widow of J.P. Marquand whose estate was allied financially with the Averill Harriman and Rockefeller fortunes.

This may or may not be true (I heard it from the Head Librarian of the Rare Book Room), but it is more than likely that the influence of Adelaide led to the daughter's being offered that summer a childcare job with the David Rockefeller family, "the gayer side," according to Paul, in one of the several letters which close the family drama of March to May, 1959.

Adelaide and Paul were lovers.

I have this gossip from the professor who hired me.

As a poet, my relation to Paul Engle is not unambiguous.

He was also the founder of the International Writing Program, also at Iowa City, and one (if not the first) book I bought after moving there, at the University Bookstore, the same month that I found Mary Engle's letters, was a small volume of poems by the Hungarian poet Attila József, translated by John Bakti and printed by Paul Engle's program.

These were the only poems that spoke to me for years, and there is a line in one of the poems (called *MAMA*) that I have decided to carry on: "Listen to this, proletarians."

May 31, 1959, Father to Daughter: "We will just have to keep our fingers crossed about mother. She has been averaging a bottle of gin a day. She may pull herself together for the week and be quite decent; and of course when she does that, she is very amusing company."

The brutality with which this information is delivered struck me as hard then as it does now, arriving at the end of a continuum that is all Mary's rollicking good will and genuine solicitation for the welfare of others.

She is often up before dawn, like a farmer, and writing while listening to what all working farmers listen to: The Farm Hour.

"It beats all get out."

Signed: Mary Engle.

She is the poet who didn't know it, a counter-punching radio, and I keep returning to the copies I made of these letters, reading them in a way that I have only now begun to be able to answer.

Signed: Mary Engle.

When I write the last name down the last two letters frequently transpose, and I find myself looking at the name of Marx's partner, *Origin of the Family, Private Property and the State*.

Mary uses multiple signs for her name, her signature: M. (which, since she always addresses her daughter as M., would indicate that she is just as often writing to herself); also B. (for Beanie, the family nickname); *ANON*. (written once only, with a stunningly beautiful calligraphic captial A); and (again, once only) "the Witch."

I began to contemplate coming out with the secret of the company I keep with this companion when, writing in the 'vicinity' of the beating of Rodney King, for me a jolting repetition of the police beating and frame-up of a young communist I knew in Iowa,

the public details of which appear in a bulletin reproduced in the final issue of *ACTS* magazine, the private details of which include the fact that I and my wife, Myung Mi Kim, were to stay with Mark and his wife, Kate Kaku—a Japanese-American whose family had been dispossessed and incarcerated during the last world war, and like Mark a communist—

the same evening (March 4, 1988) twenty-nine years and one day after Mary Engle begins her domestic chronicle, when Mark was arrested and a frame-up initiated which continues even as this book is being made,

as we were in Des Moines to attend the annual Rural Women's Conference sponsored by Prairie Fire, a grass-roots group philosophically associated with the electoral hopes of the Rainbow Coalition,

and I had been invited to speak at a panel for the Militant Labor Forum, an arm of the Socialist Workers Party (whose program clearly states the need for a Workers and Farmers government) about a recent trip I had made to Nicaragua to help with the coffee harvest and express solidarity with the Sandinistas' revolution,

and carrying this knowledge into the writing reacting against foreboding manifestations of methodical State violence, in the work of the writing, there were a few crucial words that were therefore for me when I needed them.

Tedium Drum, part four, "It was a saying of ours, a saying of ours for years, we may be goats, but we have our rights."

Signed: Mary Engle.

Months later, writing an imaginary, terrorizing nightsong to my only child, a nursery rhyme for the new monster, Riot, it was again a phrase of Mary's that came to my aid and closed the song.

Market Tender Family, "Kinderhyme": "Am sure that my copy of Little Fur Child is lost."

Signed: Mary Engle.

There are hundreds of other words of hers and parts of her thoughts littered in the lines and figuration of the work I have been writing in the last year, 1994.

These are my fragments of a liquidation, which, after the making of my first book, *TEDIUM DRUM*, accompany me to that bend in the road where a poet may greet her mentors in a free and easy way, when, to quote Zukofsky, use hardly enters into their exchanges, though Marx would add that Freedom is the appropriation of Necessity, and it is out of deep need that I bend my ear to the furious Latin, years cold as Lollards, in homage to Anonymity and the sheer force and will to live.

On the page in one of my notebooks dated 9/26/81, facing the phone number and the hour of appointment with the Professor, himself a disappointed, dissipated novelist, written with excruciating, frightened care is the following line from Shelley's *PROMETHEUS UNBOUND*:

"Most vain all hope but love and thou art far"

for Myung Mi Kim

and Malcolm Song-Ok Kim

Huge sea of sorrow, and tempestuous griefe,
   Wherein my feeble barke is tossed long,
   Far from the hoped hauen of reliefe,
   Why do thy cruell billowes beat so strong,
   And thy moyst mountaines each on others throng,
   Threatening to swallow vp my fearefull life?
   O do thy cruell wrath and spightfull wrong
   At length allay, and stint thy stormy strife,
Which in these troubled bowels raignes, and rageth rife.

For else my feeble vessell crazd, and crackt
   Through thy strong buffets and outrageous blowes,
   Cannot endure, but needs it must be wrackt
   On the rough rocks, or on the sandy shallowes,
   The whiles that loue it steres, and fortune rowes;
   Loue my lewd Pilot hath a restlesse mind
   And fortune Boteswaines no assuraunce knowes,
   But saile withouten starres, gainst tide and wind:
How can they other do, sith both are bold and blind?

Thou God of winds, that raignest in the seas,
   That raignest also in the Continent,
   At last blow vp some gentle gale of ease,
   The which may bring my ship, ere it be rent,
   Vnto the gladsome port of her intent:
   Then when I shall my selfe in safety see,
   A table for eternall moniment
   Of thy great grace, and my great ieopardee,
Great Neptune, I auow to hallow vnto thee.

                    Edmund Spenser

SPELT FROM SIBYL'S LEAVES

*Earnest, earthless, equal, attuneable, | vaulty, voluminous,
... stupendous*
*Evening strains to be tíme's vást, | womb-of-all, home-of-all,
hearse-of-all night.*
*Her fond yellow hornlight wound to the west, | her wild
hollow hoarlight hung to the height*
*Waste; her earliest stars, earlstars, | stárs principal, overbend
us,*
*Fíre-féaturing heaven. For earth | her being has unbound; her
dapple is at end, as-*
*tray or aswarm, all throughther, in throngs; | self ín self
steepèd and páshed—qúite*
*Disremembering, dísmémbering | áll now. Heart, you round
me right*
*With: Óur évening is over us; óur night | whélms, whélms,
ánd will end us.*

*Only the beakleaved boughs dragonish | damask the tool-
smooth bleak light; black,*
*Ever so black on it. Óur tale, O óur oracle! | Lét life, wáned,
ah lét life wind*
*Off hér once skéined stained véined varíety | upon, áll on twó
spools; párt, pen, páck*
*Now her áll in twó flocks, twó folds—black, white; | right,
wrong; reckon but, reck but, mind*
*But thése two; wáre of a wórld where bút these | twó tell, each
off the óther; of a rack*
*Where, selfwrung, selfstrung, sheathe- and shelterless, | thóughts
agaínst thoughts ín groans grínd.*

Gerard Manley Hopkins

COMMONPLACE

Of lollardie

how many yeres ben gon

how many fals collacioun

bok so many bei and selle

many wrong   hath wrought

many on   many an other

many a new law hath befalle

as I have go   I many and many mo

makth that ful many harm

hielde in honde   many cours

in covenable time   overtorn

cunne manyon   konne   misfar

The worldes good was ferst comune

so were it good to take

and makth the corn good chepe or dere

and kepe   (for all our trust

is on this good)   is good to kepe

Richesse upon the comun good
wher that a thyng itself is good
that it were good to make

        some good tidinge
        good hiede toke

torne it to good
torn it to harm

        good to ben al on

How that he mihte his cause availe

so mai them knowe, how the florin

devise them therinne   Stand

how thei wol bidde travaile

    dede may non be
    noght longe stonde   [relesse]

That there may be no loveday   [kenne]

I stod as hene as hawk in halle

So ferr it was out of mi thoght
of what I thoghte to telle
that topulled in my thought

The worste speche
is rathest herd
Mi fader, as fer lacke
                              unloke

The lunge
upon the wrong
seith sche is siek

After the comun speche

My speche and this
obedience, lacke vois
that selve speke out

For Anger that thei se me have
towards love, for ought I can

me yit avise, I wol me noght
therof excuse,

I wol it hide, and holde me
covert alway

Thus sche desputeth in hire thoght
what thing that thanne
into my thought

(herd said that thoght is fre

　　Thoght pottes hote

That ther may be no vois
may nothing be hidd
Pite may noghte be

what as evere I thoghte spoke
I not what thing
was in my thought

There is no hope, whan in that time
in time of nede, we schal non have
that we withinne the time also

that writen of the time
for al such time of love is
the present time which now is

It souneth in here Ere

that have cause of hope
that hope scholde be

the more   toward here

Toward here   thyng   for pilage

that here Ancestre

here name schall be rad

who so is trewe of tunge

woldist thou glase the gable
and grave therin thin name

coupable (culpable)

                  aradde

That for non other

                Rescousse

        encress

a ferly—a 'wonder hap'
(to commune)

        nowther text ne glose

  [commend   commend]

      schryve

hestes

feigned thing

wher sone upon the Non he cam

     ther halp no Seil
     ther halp no Ore

a verrai Signe
              nor of non
not that if it
          now

wolde sende

and it forsoke

How ferr I stonde from grace

Bot it is an hindrere

defalte

And lost of al the comun grace

The comun vois
The comun place

of alle wommanysshe

remenant

in that spot it
sprang to that

sprang in space

that spot my honde I spenned

as blwe as ble of Ynde

wyth schymeryng schene (shimmering sheen)

rownande rounde raykande (whispering noise flowing)

glade (joyful)

glace (glide)

how fele fer yeres are gone

and fewe to come   to have grace

to go with hem   treuthe to seke

atte plow for pore mennes sake

TERRACE

Imprisoned mourned
toward a forest the face directed
round setting smooth the sides
judged gems. Set by that store

apart as singular, often have there flowed
many let to steal. Spot of spice
overspread yellow, blue and red
reproduce the more fair have grown

than the meadows and hedgerows
might suffice, every pebble
in the pool well set there,
from that spot that is speech

spirit sprang, my body mound

Scattered a few loose speeches
those speeches
whose speeches

reduced into writing

extant in writing
extant in records of pleas

from one age to another
their binding power

are not set down in writing in that manner
are of a vast extant

all those laws have their several monuments in writing

and we may find some footsteps
some Resemblance
in case she will have any

with that of Descents
with us at this day

and that the case was otherwise
in course of purchase
consonant to the law

Reward, among companions
caused to resolve

But taken from that intention

      had practiced
      not wrought
      not yet none

whose generation can recount

      Open the book
      and at that site
      no other color

abundantly supply

To fall
(from prosperity)

how far from
famishing

as unpang'd can

cull

Recompense

Ill befit
words should address

I had thought that it
was there across opposite

those supposed
were division
nowhere about

Was not a penny you
a penny per your
agreement you then
ask more

(have I the right)
apportion/share
and their labor in
result slip away

or so I thought
it was there across
opposite those supposed
division, supposed

To hope it now
in hope achieve
a hope caught
that what hope

I wait and hope
in hope that this
is cause for hope
the grace of hope

in the absence of specific formulation
construction of a sure road

aporia (literally as the
absence of any road)
methodos (a path)

To hire
and find some
in agreement we come
for a penny a day
to cut and tie
the lord said to those
Now you know
this day has no end

exert
reprove   those that worked
summons   make them assemble

           propose (make)

       mete hard
   my penny have justly
           taken here

                                   forfeited
       statement
withstanding

for a meeting might stop
    straightway

a white line open at the sides and
trimmed with pearls, in my opinion,
pearl and no other

           [comprehend value]

           joy for a gem
                        put in a purse
                        or purpose
           at the top
       sat a child   eluded

                   beheld

cease

sought

     goods

The pearl *is* price

       amend

as in the Apocalypse
St. John saw them all
on the hill, that hill

         excuse/dispel

The third to pass this region

That believe nothing and that is

Pride. Ill befit to believe no

account be true. Words should address

treasure's cause.

Now count it.

Each tier

For the measure

plates
inscribed

                vie

a name
form
following   deficient
date

though there were many
no crowding in their array

         then awoke . and saw
           the sun in the south
        without food or money
           on Malvern hills

              dictum

             AMEN(d)

         trammel and halve

             [have]

     single petal of

                  u   p

                        Rose

VAULT

It is by crossing the seven terraces

in as many hands the manuscripts

itinerant continued by, extracted out

and you have called that Cause made for you manifestly

amicitiae, testimonies of our love

penitentiae, a strict course of life

The seed of you in every virtue

and all that mark hath made

adorned with double rows of Rose

inconverted muting far from averring

some few broken reports of those

and other acts of Power and Force

Accusable, the hand of the poet is not

above that principle which makes no regression

from privations, Moiety

divided not by the sea, or any considerable arm

gnaw'd out of graves, our skulls

made into drinking bowls transplant

antipathies the more authentic which acknowledge

their effects, and to this effect

many injunctions were afterward admitted

only a gentle and continued covenant to one another

in succession, we in twynne

descents to Bastard *eigne*

The lords have great weight and authority in declaring

usage and the many revolutions

revers'd by error, especially bold

that reaffirm the dignity of learning

for the English poet also, and in the next age

if historical time is stinted, attenuable or confined

Beauty of bodies much abridged

every manuary trade a specious prize

It is the Plowman, whose incarnation

you cannot touch with tropes

nor balance on blocks of type

five hundred ten and five

Set, without certain footing

increase grains welling where else each good

could flourishing, overspread. Preserved

they are grown into use ensuing

as fair congruity as the secular

languors which accompany effusion

in a festival time, gravel when on that ground

advanced from a base estate

vehement sudden onset of argument, reason

reproduce there was imprisoned some letters

shew'd as mine importing hate

abolished the dulcet part

Tenets

not well considering the assertion of

impelling forward

station, for such as termed

without inflexion, alternity or vicissitude

I would ask you plainly roughly crude

concerning some wreck which we have gotten into

as before now the cannonadings have

taken off into something like an echo

in and out of whose arches the aerial mist

even in overthrow, from the Canadas

glided nigh

His name for the writing was the *Queen*

that rides on a glassy sea, a glass ship's

glass sailors in the rigging's spun glass

a glass dog and glass axe, glass eyes

of the glass captain with glass cigar

glass spars glass seahorses and dolphins carved

the crash and its imprecations, exponent.

A young man in a workman's blue blouse

colored and then grinned

in a grimace of welcome.

The light is political-poetical

The passage boat plies twice

[for Aaron Shurin

The Paris transcriber

with one stroke on the keyboard made it read

like a literary critic and (social democratic)

commentator, one of those writers

who have committed themselves to the Cause

and started writing on the side of the Cause

that weighs, and its weight, its absence, what it is *not*

I am grateful to the keeper of Western Manuscripts

for permission to quote from the late professor

whose head dropped heavily on the boards

unmasked, unmistakeable when you studied

servilities in a letter, with a foreign stamp

An den Festungsgefangenen Herr Toller:

Here is no weakness, no effects of prison.

Klassenstandpunkt (class analysis) my pallet.

I'm writing on it, individualized, in the grey

stone building wet and cold. For days it has rained.

I am close to you, as close to you

as one who has fallen asleep in a meadow

a cell with walls papered with printed copies

tin cups full of the national importance

set down, that plenary pardoning power

reciting not the remotest promise

for authors of their own misfortune

What's expiated? asked the child

Our English endured for many miles

the work of one scribe writing a fine Anglicana Formata

forty leaves of which have been removed

for their illuminations, each the shape

and size of brick, my Brecht, the model book

cast across with stones as though

a replica were floating whole,

like an ox in a contracted field

or Lowell girls the rows of looms

pressed home by hard facts. The scene

cannot be located, and the stage is vast

Set them all in a row

stack each like a penny

that counted all day

and all the more often

that often have waited

in common, belonging

to the time of the day

at evensong, one hour

before the sun goes down

Count them at last in full

that often have waited

and are not set free

FREEHOLDS

Overswaying enforced
no opener, insufficient

fraud and fallacy was
used, in which delivery

mistook, or traduced
mendacities, temptations

from the Object itself
had example and deter

although their intellectuals
had not failed in theory

performances dismissed
with censure, considering

the common interest

Of penance my plough
how the prest preued no pardoun
Biennales and triennales and

from contemplation plunged

degree bids cleanse with dew
in the perimeter where is narrow

        [... in sheer rage tore it in two

scrupulous remnant

snapped forc   *ch*

                    chaffare (buying and selling)

Metropolis (the brain)

the poysoned Belly brake. Snakes

speak out of the spinal marrow

ensample
Discourse allow excursion

                        collaterall truths

if we sometimes take wide liberty, we are not single,
but erre by great example

                seldom without some extremity

Some commendable venemous
                                salute
stands saluted
with hard language
                [maniples?]

Wee enter into a newe, a nerrer bond
exculed [exculcated?]
                        leave of discourse of
                        disabilitee
                                [incrassated?]

That the danger of breaking them should stray us
from making them.

Certaine impediments being removed any may walk
the way without stumbling.

Not of an Ox
and of musick also the note
nice customes
and the liberties that followes

it were an endlesse thing
(it were an englysshe thing)

spek't in a womans key
like such a woman
as any of us three

the beakes of Ravens
and pecks of Crowes
give us the bones

then a Doves motion
counter reflect

wheat then not threshd
[threash] none winnow

Vault to every
wrong transported

Take some note
chappell them

That of the noise
and of the sound
that hath the voice

The song is set
voice and sound
of instrument

                    honored wife
              in assemblage love thrives
bring that bear this pearl
discourse in passage

On their foreheads written
that of that song
that company

Barr'd
underprop

to find
and fasten

or quicken
though we have kept them long

in their proper
houses, or boxes

where some have lived
The like discoverable

those plain
and unquestionable

unlimited bounds

enlarged with the latitude
yet to secure

either abrogate
or alter

Consider how many hundred lines
there are

Consider how many thousand severall
words have been

carelessly and without study composed
out of 24 letters

let a Painter carelessly limn
out a million

I have seen a Grammarian towr
over a single line

and breathing sometyme
their auditory

consonant to one another
in the Series

                              [for Michael Palmer
                              Iowa/Winter 1986

Dear M,

Some riseings
   there have been
in London of the

   Anabaptists,
fift Monarchie men
   and others,

but soon suppresd
   and 13 Executed;
Upon the King's letter

   5 of our Aldermen
were put out wch
   had got in in the

usurpers time in other
   mens places [...]
Yesterday was an humiliation

   and fast kept to
divert the Judgments
   of God upon us

and our Posteritie for
   the Abominable murther
of King Charles the first,

and is by Act of
Parliament to be kept
yearly on that day

forever. Ned is at
Cambridge and Nancy
still in London

since shrovetides
with hir eye fixed
upon one object

many howres, and noe other
hath bin by fittes
some 3 or 4 moneths

observable
salt
sallow

4.27

prohibited abettor

this the second

refuted pursued

translating her

extenuating her

to excuse the Fact

strictest minoration

degenerated inception

colorable integrities

better dispute cognition

deludable he played

forbidder. contriver.

We have declared ourself in a language

(at least probably hoping)

Pardon of the Attempt

(as if it were yet extant)

constrained to stand against

Authority drawn from the scrip

scarce named any Author whose name I do not honor

as if detraction could invite

Critical Discoursers, the shell and obvious exteriors

to add according to the custom of the Ancients

(their sober promotions)

or under any name obtain a work

(deceptible condition)

originals once removed

and that not in visible apparition

although we have free will

disadvantage of delusion

obtruded conceptions

debilitated

doubt,
Menace
ocular

(APOLLO)

who saw
that all
he made
was good

In eternity there is no distinction
of tenses

To make a revolution every day is the nature
of the sun
                    it cannot swerve

in a circle or longer way

The low and abject condition of the person
for whom so good a work was set on foot

as to stand in diameter

civility of my knee, my hat and hands

without a reel or stagger

deny priority

laugh me out of the Philosophy
laugh me out

whose actions are not begot

and with a gross rusticity admire

the homage we owe for being *least*

Sir, I return you this in acknowledgment,
and though I cannot boast of my science
in this kind, who set out not many months

since, and cast my Symbol with the rest,
yet I esteem'd it pardonable at least,
and in so general a catalysis of integrity,

to importune you with this the proplasma
and delineation of my design, wch, to avoyde
the infinite copying for some of my curious

friends, I was constrain'd to print, though
I have drawn it rudely in loose sheets,
in no small abhorrency of those painted

and formal projections of our Cockney
plotts, wch appear like pasteboard
and March pane, wherein neither cost

nor words had bin wanting, but languadge
very much. As for news of London,
it is thought by degrees most will come

to conformitie; the County hors came
hither to joyn the Regiment of foot
of this Citty, a feast at the new hall,

generall contributions for a feast for
the Poor, a long and solemn service at
Christ Church beginning at 8 a Clock

and with a sermon ending at twelve,
masts of ships and long stageing Poles
already set up for becon bon fires,

speeches and a litle play by the schollers
in the Market Place, an other by young
Cittyzens at Timber hill on a stage,

Cromwell hangd and burnt every where,
whose head is now upon Westminsterhall,
together with Iretons and Bradshows.

If it should happen that I go away
retracted for which I recall that in
this aggravated space without prejudicing
what it was that its agent heard,

that while we are daily whirled on by the swing
and mockshow, singling out
an Angle wedge of Elbow of Brittain
whereby the body may be the better moved

against the insolencies and usurpations
which extend themselves as wide as the many
exigencies in the distribution of Justice

[in the society of all who suffer under it]

Determinations and final judgments
overwrought, observable rudiments
there are hereof, prohibits all proceeding

[yet these are the parts to which it is contiguous]

Verbum indicabit, all must be resolved
per primam reritatem
most commonly called the Common Law
or,

History of the last year
applied to particular places
and some to particular causes
Lex Communis or *Jus Communis*

in what diminutives the plastick principle
impressions the colourishing
Truth dispense, who would be content
as the fittest to receive

that doctrine clapt in amongst the miracles
that the poor believed,

Communis indigentia est societatis vinculum (mutual
necessity is the surcingle of the world)

which was by transcription successively corrupted
any singularities therein correspondent
unto the private conception of any

and in the long course which has elapsed
the troops of error have too rashly charged

[upon the rhetorick of their miseries]

Wheat and Rye will grow
tender brains and pulses
as to make over that ever
from the same corculum or little original

My prayers go with the husbandmans
and those of his condition
may be as incapable as
hopeless of their reparations

It was penned in such a place
and with such disadvantage
that (I protest) from the first
setting of pen to paper

the privacy of my condition, and unequal
abilities (as I have declared) shall no further
father ardor of contention opposing
unwary understanding

Coda

A gods name see the lysts and all things fit
as when we come to love a person for their work
as the reader loves passionately the writer
for the work the writer had done

The writer has done
that they would not have done, or desired undone
as desperately as before had been done
uncivilly, as great injustice as deceiving

Responsibility did not equivalence refer facility

in the fruition enjoying have
received elation, indulgence,
whose ways are boundless, and confess

decollation of annihilated Mercy
fervent and zealous
in the halcyon days

Potentes potenter tormenta patientur

I can see nothing (the thing
well weighted) that any may
well call their own, all the
remnant of that borrowed ware
strait accompt, enhancing
vesture of innocence more
glorious than cloth or gold.

At Paules Crosse, Junii 6th, 1602. Mr Barber,
his text Luke 9, and the last verse, "Noe man that
putteth his hand to the plough and looketh back is
apt to the Kingdome of God."
[No on putting on the (his) hand on a plow
and looking at the things behind fit is for
the kingdom of God]
No man, having put his hand to the plough,
and looking back, is fit for the kingdom of God.

RECENT EVENTS

WHILE THIS GAME OF CHARITY WAS YET AT ITS HEIGHT

"As in appearance he seemed a dog, so now, in a merry way, like a dog he began to be treated. Still shuffling among the crowd, now and then he would pause, throwing back his head and opening his mouth like an elephant for tossed apples at a menagerie; when, making a space before him, people would have a bout at a strange sort of pitch-penny game, the cripple's mouth being at once target and purse, and he hailing each expertly-caught copper with a cracked bravura from his tambourine. To be the subject of alms-giving is trying, and to feel in duty bound to appear cheerfully grateful under trial, must be more so; but whatever his secret emotions, he swallowed them, while still retaining each copper this side of the oesophagus. And nearly always he grinned, and only once or twice did he wince, which was when certain coins, tossed by more playful almoners, came conveniently nigh to his teeth, an accident whose unwelcomeness was not unedged by the circumstance that the pennies thus thrown proved buttons."

Melville/*The Confidence Man*

ADJUNCT

[Quod licet Jovi
non licet bovi

1.

The coinage
I am entitled
to is small,
only the one

down the road
to whom I must
give a false
smile should he

be in the water
there, in the air
here made of
wood, dappled

purple doors
brass handles
with keyholes
a piece of

polished floor
There will I sit
carted to study,
indispensable but

not demanding, not
to be done without
and aware of that
I stand before you

without possessions
or suitable Bible
quotations, the Ox
that took the blow

2.

It is the same
as if the price
was definiteness
of form to fixed

and circulating
capital, a title
to value here
fitted high and bare

3.

Money the exiting
factor, the thing
that throws you out
Driving and being

driven, the clock
in the castle tower
Horses pull Apollo
The feet are all off

4.

It must put paid
to the notion of
repute, nor gain
for the inscriber

who will pay
for everything
pretended, this
dates from that day

5.

Exchange
heavy, the sagging
chair well cared
for parallel

survives,
took money
the way out
light and dark

6.

It is a material
scale, volume,
value, piecemeal

stipulated time

an iron works
component parts
of the constant
embodiment, unit

The substance
and magnitude

fluent
samples of the same

What is equivalent

Each of these
its properties

triangle, altitude

AUTHOR

There is no answer
for a liberty regarded as right and property

or a language that would deliver its objects
as concepts

Experienced prisoners
have explained to me a way to fight the camera

There is a five minute interval between the house
and train

BOOK

Swung to an instinct
and saw that it was common

Round dollars roused
this much in touching regard

The county of Kent
compounded, stood bound

Chief among these places
are the chains

EQUATOR
           [Arp: Art is fruit

She asked for Max the Dutchman
alongside Marx discoursing
the round world over
rotating into depth
its most distant glimpse
and grimmer, trees
that ignite at sunset
guarded by birds that spit

PROUDHON

Utopia is a picture
in a museum the viewers
pass through on their way
to a reason for being there
at all, a hole in that wall
upraised contingents
closed off
The premise
"We enter elections and we are lost"

BANNER

Riots the more miraculous and surprising
the less theoretical their foundation
or the pathos in the persons of the unemployed, begging's
lacerating implacability
lyrical in every language
the Voltaire of *Poème sur le désastre de Lisbonne*
like Leopardi, born of carnage

DEMONSTRATIONS HAVE BEGUN

Kommentarstruktur
(commentary-structure)
a form of longing for
theory (*Begriff* rather
than *Idée*) a statement like

Was wir wollen (What we want)
received by the decisive
construction that seeks itself
in the cage of the concept,
a position taken up

In the syllogism
pure thought, a fictive
being torn between
determinate judgments
i.e. "the flag is red"

One sided terms
windswept, accede
one of them having wound
a scarf round, inciting
undeterred

ECCLESIA MILITANS

Marxist doctrine
(freedom of will,
Hegelian and post-Hegelian
innocence) analysis
(*oeconomia* in Ambrose and Jerome)
—a way of life (and, as fiction
with Rousseau, the resource
"sincerity"

The author's
experience: the blinding, hieratic towers
ridentem dicere verum (truth laughingly told) Horace
an almost classical need
in the face of this freedom
as formulated, *festum stultorum*
fatuorum or *follorum*, that faith in the irrefutability
of the "document"

DURKHEIM'S DICTUM

My experience
derives from
an exposition,

a commentary
narrated in the sections numbered one to four,

a sequence of events that lend themselves
at every step, constrained to plead its calling

under the heading "documentation" incarnating
metamorphoses of Prometheus, their dark arcana
determining the themes of this didactic art—

to see in the blow a sign, brutally lit

verdict of guilt and gift of a glass eye

INTERPRETER
                    [for Steve Abbott

Stand up from the dead, the dead works
in my trouble saying arise
my only portion, disquietments
ill and absent from the ordnance

They fear we come with new and dangerous opinions
the sum of whose days spent in a room
struck dumb by the authority of
books, fare thee well then and cry for your mother

This is a word that
(if there is a heaven)
there will be an author for

The poor child gives her
money to a poorer child
This is phrased as a simple faith

[Variant]

This day was brought news of that
and much distracted, thoughts rising
stand up from the dead, from dead works

and those loose stragglings into other things
my only portion, prevalency
in my trouble saying arise

much disquietments
These things open a gap to unbelief
and savor of its sweetness in a manner

ill and absent from the ordnance
So that my spot
is not that spot

DIRECTIVE

Rights, carrots.
Misty-eyed missionaries,
hard water mineral stains.
Mellifluous lawyer's hand,

the ganglion. Rita Lewis,
Local 50, Recording Secretary
(Swift Plant in Marshalltown):
"We are our nation's conscience"

Curious as to the logistics of this
talked with Lynn last night after
the Rochester meeting, pitch
about the importance of books

entailed a film projector and someone
who knows how to run one. Transition
or confluence, in the prison of proletarian
appellation, next to no health care

and no education, plenary proposals
what caucuses are for, international
collaboration to commemorate
'Days of Decision' flood the plains

STAMPEDE EFFECT

[for Charles Olson

Work on a share basis
You learn to live with a lot less
We have a common interest
If you don't love the sea ... I don't know
If there ain't a fucking fish
Ten years won't be enough
Now we know what a fisherman is
Reading must have been hard work for him
as he muttered quite loud as he read

It is a fight to win what can be won
49 words and when and where
Youth who have organized and marched
around the hearings, the death of the sailors on the USS
Stark, the pitch to join
a less than adequate instrument, during those years
I learned to study with an almost
Talmudic care, utilizing each escalation
The product of a conscious effort

PASTOR

Rising nationalism, for example, or the viability
of appeals to contribute regularly each Sunday,
a plea to private conscience. There are no militants
in the church, only charity. What can be ascertained

as to what is needed that they may obtain,
unfortunate and tenuous employment and reward
wages bring, churches in the center of every town.
There are no funds for their emergency.

Farmers used to drive their livestock here,
and one remembered once the evening train,
and an even rarer thing, a section of track

that crossed at 90 degrees, like a small *t*.
What we have to do is find a place,
like a store, only everything is free.

THE MYTH OF THE RURAL

Not for the least necessity nor increase
of commodity, fruition and plain beholding
must the lowest far surpass in land

that tremble remembering as soon hove all
temper and proportion, thought enters once
unsitting in the sight of that great person

whose tenant appeared and pleaded for
the public soul, varying in form from other
parcel relapsing too remote conjectures

for ditcher, for digger, till deltas
wonderful tormentings, bedabbled with dirt
heavily and unremittingly pressed down

the troubled path that led them
to the city from their native fields
from the work of their hands to Rhetoric

THE KITCHEN IN KING'S CROSS ROAD

Two long hours

give it the intonation of an answer

give it appearance
of an ordinary life

several copies of what I thought was a person,
masterpieces to admire

Only the end of the meal was missing

favored to lift my eyes from the page

though I know too little about cooking

The rest of the day
is called the afternoon

PENINSULAR

With the historian,
the scholar, the proof

in what is read then with
such love, the threshold

to friendship
that reading is

to go to the work
as to a foreign city

Carolingian, even if the notes
refer to Rome

QUEEN OF THE AIR

[for Kathleen Fraser

around herself
the swirling glance
and not far away

great traffick and opulency
of that mighty citty
this was wrote in 1714

soon after pirated
cry'd about the streets
in a half-penny sheet

some way or other
to inform the reader
as if by the wayside

the two were returning
to Rome still a few
miles away, a crossroad

from the latin day
pictures hung on a long, low wall
as if free to enter

and rest for awhile
she held the door
for her companion

the house of song
quiet stealth
expressiveness

her early essays
and special sympathies
incongruity anew

MIRROR MIRROR ON THE WALL

I would become that constant endeavor to speak
personally that all
might acquit me

of masculinity
which personality
precludes all possibility

of fulfilling employments
in Dante's hell, those lords of song
share the light & air

MALEVOLENCE

Now who is the father of lies?

slighting of her speech now the eye

that despises the mother the ravens

peck out and eat

II

PLUME

There is only the mother

The town and the river
The faces of passers-by

I can't keep what I took, only leave you

That woman was only
a laborer

The turning-days
slip by

PAINT BOX

Nobody likes things the way they are
Wait till your asked

You have to feel the place
out first, accountability

and the immediate task
One of the disappointments

accepted, one of the many.
Sunflowers. Paroxysms.

What mattered. I can't
tell you how.

PORCELAIN

My fascination with Marcel's Francoise

The lie, in elementary school, when asked
what she was

an unlettered woman

In 1967 I was obliged to identify
my mother as my maid

(her uniform)

JUNK

That the *Communist Manifesto* was included among
the few books that belonged to an aircraft sheetmetal
worker and a grocery store worker, the entire catalogue
consisting of a Modern Library edition of Robert Frost,
a volume of patriotic ballads by Eddie Guest, *God's
Trombones* by James Weldon Johnson, *Huckleberry Finn*
and *Tom Sawyer, The Wind in the Willows, The Story of Sioux
County, The World's Great Philosophies* and *The Best Loved
Poems of the American People,* was due to the one year
my mother was able to attend a South Dakota teacher's
college, and my father's brief exposure in Los Angeles
to the labor movement in the 1930s. Upton Sinclair was
the family martyr—for what he had done, not what he'd
written. The only church we ever attended were my
mother's stories of growing up on the farm. I introduce
this bibliography the more concretely to insist that I read
everything, and everything I read I took.

PEN PAL

My hands look as horrible as usual but they do not hurt
at all
uncomely

under call
the duty
here, to spare

a word
awareness
slaves die

like dogs
a Syrian
the stroke

caught
above
the ear

PILGRIMAGE

[for Susan Gevirtz

Mr. Spicer rose. She made a note
as Mr. Spicer spoke,

cries came through the open window
as if police were hauling someone
along the street against their will

Not that I would not have found my way without you,

head gripped by gin, pen dipped in crud.

Meals together as an occasion for conversation
with the children,

a chorus of voices, country people
going home

DEAR VALLEJO

[expressionistical
analystical
mystical

joskin

(country bumpkin)

From this day on you begin
your history,

(might have made it out to be
the shadow of her smile)

I was encouraged by something, mother,

I thought I couldn't know
whether it was a prosperous
nation or not, and whether
I was in a thriving state or not,
unless I found out who had got
the money, and whether
any of it was mine.

PENNY LABOR

["Where some father says
your words are not connect"
Michael Palmer, *SUN*

infected
mitigate

Now to make up for a little of what we owe

holding out one hand

sobers up those

axioms, idioms

what learned

(learn) what

hated (I hated)

that despotic

lack

MARY ENGLE'S ENGELS

In the expository series that carries the title
Reproduction,

presupposing, in theory at least, the possibility
of free choice,

an irrational hiatus
(hysterical) double
production in the vast
frontier between real history and the Marxist test.

Is there a theory of history? It is a fictive choice.

privative form

(thought it partly
true to the letter
of what she wrote)

DEAR ELLEN

After three months induction
into the monuments of Political Economy

bracing ourselves with a class analysis
against the indoctrination of the State,

I dreamed we were guests of the Federation
of Cuban Women,

and might even become the poet

from that grim Scots school
off the icy coast of Fife

ADMONITION

Patricia's dream
"in my sleepless state"
The waitress and her tables
The tables multiply
divided by a highway

I learned a few things from Pat, actually,
1. her dream
2. her remark
the same morning, on the eve of her new job
at the Swift packing plant,

You have to organize from where you are, what you are

Enact that affirmation, Tony Dutrow quoting Kipling's *If*

Our farm: chickens for laying and meat
           goats for milk, cheese and meat
           a pig or two, for the pork
           and the garden, serious work

NOTES FOR DUGDALE'S HISTORY OF
EMBANKING AND DRAINING, 1662

over this made and wide
drainings, semeings and cuttung[s] cutt

"of whom in the meantime
present my true respects"

defray

& magnify god in the night & my dark bed

& when the four aclock bell awaked mee

          a sighing sound

cold water poured out of a jug

JOSEPH

Walking along the road, watching the tractor climb
the hill.

Walking along the road, watching the tractor
climb the hill. She went to town to work each day.

He worked in the mill. All the men in the town
worked in the mill.

There was a track and a station.

      The tractor climbs the hill
      a mile back down the road.

          out of sight up the road

a mile beyond
the top of the hill   back down the road
beside the barn   two days back down the road
beyond the fence

          the day, the road, the heat
        the lane turns from the road
        more quiet than the road

ahead to where the road curves on and away

It was at the edge of town
where the street became a road

The street curved into the gravel road

One place the same as another

This place or that place
what word it used as a name

about a half mile away

       increasing definition

soybeans in the bottom land
corn along the edge of the hills

in another time
must have occurred
to another person

a tree beside the road

they went away across the pasture

went through the barn
the stalls all wide open
the roof full of holes

the big cow and
the little calf

we went down the hill

we went up the hill

the cows came out of the barn

we went on past the barn

some birds on the barn door

The cows came out
of the barn
The cows ran up the hill
The cows ran down the hill
We went toward the barn
up the steep hill
at the top of the hill
we saw the steeple
We looked back down
the hill. We went on
past the barn
and thru the gate
at the foot of the
hill. I came up from
the field along the
fence I went along
the fence. We went along
the fence caught on a nail
till we got back to
the barn
We went thru the barn
the stalls all wide open
No straw on the floor
We went around the barn
The big and

BRECHT'S MARIA

[after Zukofsky

The night
when she
first gave

birth had
been cold
but years

later she
forgot all
about the

frost in
the sagging
beams and

the smoking
stove and
the spasms

towards
morning
above

all she
forgot
the bitter

shame
common
among

the poor
of having
no privacy

that was
the main
reason why

years later
it became
a holiday

for all to
take part in
the shepherds'

coarse chatter
fell silent
later they

turned into
the kings of
the story

the wind
which was
very cold

turned into
the singing
of angels

and all
that was
left of

the hole
in the roof
that let

in the
frost was
the star

THE DIGGING STICK

The emotion will wear off, ruined by the rent.

It was a page from history, as far as I could see.

Attached, that it should prove worth the slurring over.

There is no aim, no exertion, too much rain and mud
and must spare my eyes, they get weak and inflamed.

Rendered tepid, or I can't write—can't fix the time—
detailed relations of events but lately passed.

The garden gate opens on the towing path.

The sun pouring in, luxurious conveyances

a long way from everyone.

By the extremity of our situation
we were cut off from customary forms.

Dictates, or demonstrances to that effect.

We began to experience, not understanding
and ate and drank mechanically.

One day the child had come to him and said
"Open your mouth. I want to see your heart."

The sight of a pen, a suppressed stanza
doubly welcome, no matter by what course.

With the help of our German Master
nach kur, and this is a pretty place,
a short mythological comic drama
which must be bunglingly made.

The tongue must touch the roof of the mouth,
house, housed the teeth must also manipulate,
pry and press restitution, words are much larger
than we are, I had to tell him, spiral odor of
nickel and ice or canyon and crayon lacing
key district, precinct, precept, peregrination.

What was three o'clock and suddenly not, a simple
task. Bright, brief intent. The sour taste of a wasted
hour, waxing. Assailed, it was inevitable and will
continue as was customary with the Bible during
the Middle Ages, that the misreadings arrive like
a cryptography. The treasure of the twelfth letter of
the alphabet. A bulky volume, coarse. What to make
of the admonitions. A gown of honor and a crown
of honor. The gown she took untorn, the crown intact.
We walk along walking about with those just walking
about or waited at the corner for the bus. In the immense
clearing someone is still moving. I went with them
to a reception at the Cuban embassy, in honor of
the anniversary of their revolution. *Ich bins genant*
ein ackerman, von vogelwat ist mein pflug.

Sick of the sound of them next door throwing a ball, the height of the chair not high enough for the desk's unhappiness, vagaries, vagrancy, vacantly a spot is waiting. The ball hits the fence. The ball goes over the fence, the continent, will you ever learn Spanish, all these wishes momentous, monstrous. The wind picks up in the late afternoon, the effort it takes to turn a page. Not to mention make a note of something, anything. Subordinated, concentric. My excitement with Anat's method, is it her training? Architecture. Identifying a project, a series of experiments or explorations, emotion in the emerging concept, expanding a problem by ennumerating its many sides. Struck today by how much Vallejo there is in Che. The chair is too low. This is a thought that keeps coming back, and my wrists have nowhere to rest. It appears as though the steak will defrost in time for dinner. At least the kitchen is large enough to walk around in and that's not true of the other rooms. What does it mean when you think, "I need a drink." The child just woke up. It is time to stop. One does not arrive. Not even another language can drag you out, rinsed clean and dry. Horizon word. *Es el reloj. En la selva de los relojes.* Wound of an hour, a darkening tower. *El reflejo es lo real. Lo real es lo reflejo.* A new stage begins today. *Cuerpo, recuerdo.* Sheep and cattle ticks, gnats, mosquitoes. *Amanacer.* A day of little or no progress, or mobility. Motionless, under duress. *Todo transcurre en la madrugada.* I had the chills all day, but the illness did not overtake me. *Pero no se pudo precisar por cierta inseguridad.* A slow and laborious day, a day of calm and replenishing. A day of quiet, a lost day. *No tiene mas que maiz.* There is nothing else to do but go back, physically weaker day by day. *Como el trigo es tierno. Como una sombra de oro en el trigal.* Encirclement, the mountains. The various aspects of the many folded hills. A desk in the corner of an open room, a family room. The blank plain across which one becomes exposed, partial views. Binoculars. Two large pink roses are in bloom outside. The windows are streaked, a film impossible to rinse away. Without hope, I wrote last night. Not that I have any interest in (to quote Vallejo) "my personal experience." The great difference between 'trigo' and 'maiz,' for example, though the typewriter cannot make accent marks. A new erasing ribbon is needed as of now.

First this and that
what happened

to the red cap
This is exactly

all I know
The notch in the door

How much damage
will we have to pay for

and we need that money
The soup needs stirring

All the while I thought
he would be waking up

and all he asked for
was a glass of milk

and couldn't stay awake
for even that

What happened
to his cap

Stupidity, a scar, can start
—denotes spot—activity
muscles stirring—obstacle—
futile, thwarted play, a child's

first questions—no answer—
hidden pain, in motion
repeatedly leaping, a dog
at the door—giving up—

renewed attempts, the child's
attention—balked—insensitivity
the scar—a spot—calloused,
stifled urge, deformities

apt to form—endured—forbidden
boldness, forbidden tears
—intelligence—the snail's horn,
smells its way—an injury—

TROPHY

What is upheld as Beautiful
is what is unreal, these bonds
are broken only on the job

where the male is called
a 'commie,' and the female
is a 'commie whore'

Woman an available wedge
and the child becomes alienable
like everything else

BULLETIN

March 4, 1988 was an uncommon day in the life of Mark
Curtis. That afternoon, around 2:00 p.m., a group of
Hispanic workers at the Swift-Monfort packing plant where
Mark also worked had spontaneously walked off the job in
protest against management's refusal of their request to
attend a meeting. The meeting they wanted to attend had
been called by Hispanic community leaders and involved
the INS, Swift Management, the press and the public in an
emergency response to the March 1st immigration raid at
the Swift plant where 16 Mexicans and 1 El Salvadoran were
handcuffed and led away by federal agents in the middle of
their shift. The walkout was dramatic. Every minute on the
assembly-line meant tens of thousands of dollars, and the
company quickly gave in to the workers' demands. They
scheduled a second meeting at 5:00 p.m. Mark attended this
meeting, and participated in discussions, speaking in
Spanish, about building a demonstration the following week
to protest the immigration raid and the abuse of the rights
of the Swift 17, as they soon came to be called. An even
greater challenge was posed by the racial divisions within
the workforce in the plant and the necessity to win the
white and black 'American' workers over to the side of the
Hispanics. The question of immigrant labor is sensitive.
Many workers are prejudiced not only along race lines, but
against the fact of immigration itself as the source of the
disappearance of 'American' jobs. One major responsibility
of a conscious revolutionary is to work to support the
strength of the union in the solidarity of its rank and file
membership, a unity impossible to attain when workers are
divided by their competition against each other for jobs.

III

ADDRESS

To the Poets

To the Prosecutor

To the Parole Board

To the City of Des Moines

[To a Working-Man]

To a Woman Reader

To my Wife and Child

To the Three Children Who Sent Chocolate and Flowers

To the Young Socialists

To Professor Marcuse

To 'Poor' B.B.

1.

"Brecht found me in the garden
reading." (Walter B.) "We found
Korsch on the first floor of a
boardinghouse. His English also
had a hard sound.
                    As we reached
America we saw from the deck all
those who had come to welcome
Brecht. A little later, there
was a knock on the door.
Brecht was standing there."
(Ruth Berlau)

2.

The Monday after the Friday Mark was
handcuffed, booked, interrogated, his
face—the left cheekbone shattered—

what began on the shopfloor, immigration
raid, cops—the beating—and ended
(am not sure whether it ended) with

this wanting to write to, address, write
'about' or towards something like this
excruciating, hallucinatory, Real.

3.

Reproduction, a social relation
glut (a dime a dozen) bare minimum
*Kovtun, "Stepanova's Anti-Book"
in *Surface to Space*, Stepanova

followed this in 1919 with her
handmade book *Gaust Chaba*
consisting of collages and made
in an edition of fifty copies

4.

The quarters of the globe
copper and copper-fastened

far more likely the copy
than the copying clerk

The century in which a book
appears

its predominant
defect

1.

The question of a chronological site.

It would not even be to document the trace of
a transformation (nothing external was changed)
But: "What it takes to win the workers' ears"

At the plant gate,
the threat of violence. Exposure, vulnerability.

To delineate the communist as prototypically
'feminine' in its construction, in a political
sphere of prejudice, censure, domination.

(That maniac at the trial threatening her
with calling the cops

2.

An hour-long lecture each day, from only a few notes.

Mary-Alice Waters, editor, *New International*:

" . . . whether the increasingly frequent
wars following as they do a relatively
peaceful period are to be regarded as

'accidents' or 'episodes' or whether
they are to be seen as the first signs
of an even greater confrontation . . . "

For, apart from politics,
or in politics, apart from
the scholar, the latter, delimit
the 'place' of Purpose
onlooking set down

3.

For Mac, experience stood as authority,
hence his fondness for maxims and proverbs
(social speech)
                    'footloose and fancy free'

(as if knowledge was simply an instrument for
our activity)

Suspicion in the Party
of the Imaginary, "Delusion," "Speculation," etc.
Instances of this.

Or, in response to a question
about Jesse Jackson and the larger
problem of parlimentary reform:

"The road to hell is paved
with good intentions."

4.

The last I heard of Kate she was in New York
on the National Committee. In a bar called "The Mill"
on Mark's birthday, the gift of my copy of József
and Jim Daniels' *Places/Everyone*.

"This is an experience we can all identify with,"
Mark said, reading aloud at our table
Jim's poem about waiting
at the plant gate to be hired.

That because of this experience, Mark's
experience, there can be no turning back.
The severity of my attraction based on the
life they lived. Their dedication (Jewish
in their underground vocation, their obedience
to the Book).

Jabès: "The Jews know that it is not enough
to believe in a truth, that we must, each time,
deserve it. There is no merit but in the stubborn
effort to reach it."

from this point on...

1.

Protracted

while the ear, that

taken in tones as

light from a miner's

lamp, despite the

hindrances and tend

2.

By the concurring

steps of a like use

here, prevaricate

shunning tidings

appointed to pull

the absent oar

3.

Retained as an infinite occurrence

on setting a purpose

the light of doctrine

a kind of magnitude

Prudence approve the step

or stem

4.

inflammatory

and study

dumb-thumbed pages

"and my voice did not obey me"

left in a state of visible agitation

(station)

1.

Little
directly but
sea between
your house

and Iceland
conceived to
resound the
voices at

their shows
and clank
the king's
chains

2.

Revert
to my devotion
having made
no effort

On my body
marks remaining
manuscript
every scrap

committed fault
prevent my name
monotonous
& delayed

3.

Must this also
remain unfinished
unable to be continued
recumbant, barring

even the error, not
even the inevitable
terror in which writing
is held, susceptibility

or at least the thought
that the choice was free
Must this also remain
unfinished

4.

Rowers
had kept
intact
unceasing

The mud, the mine
would not wish themselves

The preliminary step

(neither 'unequal' nor 'thwarted'
but "uncertain"

Bewilderment, widespread

whereby   was action   lost

fall back

to the pallet

tired of the fever
as from coughing

compelled to
and came to an understanding

and held the value
of one

The work of
"the other side"

We were welcomed
hardly understanding

viable, denouncing

Not yet here and yet at hand

"I have come to you"

outside the emanation

a breath in the interreal

tilted

liable to be brusque

or just a stone wall

like talking to a wall

SHOWCASE

Jody, Jim Coop, Virgil, Campy, Paul
stood there unorganized

There is no law that says you should

A lesson learned by rote. He was repeating what
(what they meant was
there was no such thing)

"The imagination of the worker knows no bounds"

The simplest words
this suspicion relay

The speaker invited was denied a visa,
and later found murdered

empty-handed
union members
from all over

Did you leaflet

The shop steward
identified himself
as a component
in a hierarchy

The USDA Inspector's story
and the larger question: what is the role of a grocery
distributor?

Set up a solidarity fund

This instead of
the city's crumbs
and close-up of
the secretary

and 'dialect'
(the crystallization
of style) The
'canonization of hard work'

in the sermon literature of the time.
In the *Comedia* there is hardly ever any overt mention
of the problem of poverty and the right use of riches.
(But see the pastoral passage Bunting 'translates').

When we got to Iowa Falls it was raining hard and the
parking lot at the plant was empty except for one pickup
and someone was in it. Ellen grabbed a sub blank and a
copy of the paper and ran over to the truck and the man
opened the passenger door and she climbed inside. When
she came back to the car she said that he was a farmer
waiting to meet another farmer to go and see about some
hogs, that he didn't work at the plant, wasn't interested in
politics, but there was a place in town where the workers
hung out, a former diner someone had donated to the
union when the union had found out that the plant was
going down, this time for good. We drove over and found

the diner, in the middle of town, with a large banner stretched across the front that read DISPLACED WORKERS. We walked into the middle of a meeting. A rep from the International was talking to a group of about forty—mostly men—about workmen's comp, sick pay, and so on, and how they should expect that the company would try to screw them out of everything written into their contract. He didn't have any advice about what to do, saying that he thought it was important to know beforehand and to keep your head up and if enough happened the union would file suit and they could expect a fair hearing in court, except that the company's trump card was that it was broke and running on borrowed money in order to buy time for the boys to find new jobs. There was some laughter and somebody said, "What jobs?" I said something—suddenly, without thinking—something about IBP and how the $5.00 an hour they were paying there was less than half the standard wage, and the Rep asked me if he could ask me ('Can I ask you' he'd begun)—he wanted to know who we were there for, what organization we represented, and I said we were selling *The Militant*, a newspaper, and that we were meatpackers and members of the Socialist Workers Party. He turned to the room and told them this, it was like he was their pastor, he told them he was beginning to feel like an undertaker, that he'd been in too many rooms like this one, and it felt like a funeral, too many funerals, saying that was all he had to add. The meeting broke up, and one of the men—one of the older men—drifted over to talk. Ellen was in a conversation with one of the women towards the back. Our discussion, on the road back down to Des Moines that evening, was based on our surprise. We had been given the floor. We had been allowed to be there. More, we had been made to feel welcome there. We had been asked for news about what was going on in other towns, other locals, other plants, and we had been asked to come back.

These are a few of my favorite
things, when the wind blows,
when the sky grows cold in the coalfields
of Appalachia. These are a few of the factors
involved in my decision to drive to Detroit.
Talk, worthless talk. It is tempting to talk.
Dream strong enough to wake me at 3:00 a.m.
At work now, 8:00 a.m. Rain, and the power off.
The warehouse doors wide open, the docks empty.

What did he say, that the Company
locked them out for seven months in 1977
over a contract dispute and cleaned the lagoons
polluting the river that runs through town
under threat of being shut down, that concessions
over three dollars an hour were granted three years ago
under threat of the plant closing down, that
the ones who continued working in the plant
disassociated themselves due to disappointment,
that the rest have no idea what is going to happen,
"are in the dark."
                    INTRODUCTIONS:
"I am an unorganized worker in meatpacking
from Columbus Junction in southeastern Iowa."
Connie Dawson: "We're going back to the 30's.
We're starting from the ground up." A driver
laid off from Caterpillar in the Quad Cities,
"They are making a minimum wage worker,"
in England the pink tractor sent to Ethiopia.
Rick: "The fishermen in New Foundland"
(Pete Kennedy is going to New Foundland).
Organizing drive in New Hampton (Sara Lee)
wildcat strike. "Ran it down in the decision
to fight."

July 26. Wendy Lyons (speaking
to an audience that isn't there). Why workers
cross picket lines, traditions, with conscious use
the most resolute. Redbaiting, an appeal to prejudice.
The starting point, always, class struggle.
A one-sided war.

Just off the highway to Rochester, Minnesota
take 52 north to Route 63 (63 is Broadway).
Go north until 13th Street
and follow until 19th Avenue.
Between 9th and 10th is the
entrance to Assai Heights
on the right. Iron gates.
Drive up to the top of the hill.
The meeting is in the library.

Explore the possibility of a one-year lease.

What we are look at in the long run.

Will need a phone. General meeting tomorrow

for the women of the Maynard Church.

Starting out with initial questions.

Jim's Quik Trip in Oelwein.

Celan: *Schneefall*
Dickinson: *311*

VICINITY

1.

Inexorable, the pull towards work,

a force against which the strong dislike of it
has no effect,

also the embarrassment of having to affirm
a certain continuity.

The renewed alliance
easier to bear, a perseverance

absolute in its unconditional demand.
The greater number,

something that would have no end,
that had already set

itself in motion,
without any goal and yet more and more powerful—

as without it, what could be done
without the shock of work?

2.

Here fragility will appear as unprocessed raw
material,

the intelligible 'I' as opposed to
an empirical 'I'

that lightness the immanent
utopia of historical law,

a lyricism that must conceal itself behind
the hard outline of event,

(—the homelessness of an action,

" ... only in the lyric do these direct, sudden
flashes of substance become like lost original
manuscripts suddenly made legible ... "
                    Lukács, *Theory of the Novel*

What is a parental home?

Uncommented depiction,

irreducibly there.

3.

We got up in cold rooms untended
and tired,

all volume and emphasis and
pressure,

less than ever was there any
chance of saving,

was that a method—a social
method,

half a crown, shilling, two
six penny coppers,

and practiced it like a doctor

"Self," she wrote, the light across
the outspread prospect of her life,

"one pound five."

4.

It went on snowing

It was still snowing a dense, serious snow

I will measure exactly its duration,

a much longer period gone by

active and real things

a discerning, disconcerting
thought

a delaying phrase

an unsituated, elusive event

5.

Reading it was just as much
a part of the exaltation, that
was proof of it, the moment

when one no longer worshipped
the majesty of a piece of debris,
rather seized it then tore it apart

The freedom of pure caprice

    like a butterfly
    speech hovering

events that were more and more
curtailed this sort of penury

the exorbitant pressure of
"something is happening"

6.

It was nothing less terrible than a thought

and how from then on I kept at a respectful
distance,

applying myself like a grocer's assistant with a
curious kind of confidential ... unprejudiced
eye ...

At least we know this much, the more it became wrong

or culpable? The impression
that from then on, for the pleasure

of a rigorous judgment,

such a contact quite distant.

7.

That morning, remembering the conversation
with Nan at the Hall as the snowstorm hit Des Moines,

that his own sister was raped, *that*
was why he would stop

to help, who had heard voices bound to desolation,
anonymous misery,
                    a museum existence

as happens during blizzards

What Kate said on the stand:
"He's not aggressive enough"

I have managed to say no more
about it, to stifle the questions
about what, exactly, happened.

8.

"It makes life less boring"
Paul, on the subject
of Partywork, bathing
in Lake Nicaragua.

Our easiness with them, as comrades.

Mark's comment on the farm the week
before his arrest,

"This is a good place to raise a child."

9.

This is what threw them at one another.

To make of the birth of a child the severing
instance with the Party.

Bob, who gleefully pounced on our contradictions
with a brutality that didn't consider anything.

The form of debate, the defined ground.

Argument, his certainty of being right.

10.

The search for the scene where labor
still is.

They wanted to pay a visit. Pay it.

What happens during a strike.

Why is that a question here.

" ... an episode that is not in its place,
a sort of farce in time, a different age,
a lost and baffled fragment
of history ... "

11.

Item. Memory of the packaging of fruit.
2's, 4's and 6's. What is remarkable was
the reduction of fruit to counting. Placed
in a paper tray and wrapped in plastic.

You forgot what you were handling. It was just a thing
to fill the shelf with.

It was a false position.

12.

The laments, the accusations,
every single stroke of the pen

Misery that expands and explodes
in a burst of enthusiasm by its

triumphant appropriator,
is it ever just an idea?

13.

An absurdity thrown in like a bomb.

Eros is an instrument of the courts.
The cops can use sex to frame you.

The slogan of independence is not a class slogan.

The struggle for influence in the trade unions.

Epigones, disciples who corrupt the doctrine

in Dante where meaning is conferred upon
each event by allocating to each its place.

Then began to retrace his steps indefinitely
toward abandoned positions.

14.

The beginning of knowledge

no more than
an indication
or pure direction
or empty place

calls itself
the fear
of error

alone it is true or that the truth alone
designed to avoid the toll

go it alone
gone on alone
gone down

YOUR HONOR
                [for David Levi Strauss

Dear Police Chief William Moulder

Words are the only weapon

we have. Mark's trial date

was long ago. Two men

in uniform. The soldiers

have fun. They bade the liar

hand them one by one

false witness

the old man's gum

KAMMERJUNKER

The period of our incarceration
The period of our earthly chronicle

Dear members of the parole board the status of visitors
directly affects me as I was looking forward with all
the anticipation of a friend who wishes to demonstrate
their support and love for someone they know who is

unjustly imprisoned

the Judge never spoke

you could feel the insinuation of an undercurrent of
falsehood

an awkwardness [surmounted by agony]

lapidary, the serenity of the older comrades

the purpose in the face

YOUR HONOR

call love
into my eyes, where Love has

            what attain
            what gain
            found where

Love bring as if he brings

            when you can
            what you can

what Law bid

                        a span
            can neither end nor lend

to Love look toward, deny him ear

less sure

tell of

YOUR
HONOR

with
stone
whether
stone

four
where is
there
many

were
of his
he is
rounds

the latch
the heels
keeper
sunken down

yard
white
house
whether

piece of
at the
time they
on and on

stiff and
the heels
upstairs
"of keys"

presses
depths
of only
always

upbraided
on end
what it
unloaded

      bulge

      empty and bent

   it is torn

and hanging down

As for paper,

left by the travellers
and read,

a heap beside the cold   coal
    the cold
a heap of coal

the brightness
the shred
of paper

The shed

       along past these

an exercise in recollection twelve steps off

Again, the wish, the will, to put a *class* stamp
on it,

unlike the memory of her brown polyester pants,
the zipper on the side, how they would slide off.

MINION

[March 4, 1988, Rural Women's Conference

Trade
a parade
of words
Tirade, Omaha, Kansas City, St. Louis, Chicago,
Minneapolis. Every city sent someone. The light
in the room. Sundown. This is John's room. His room
a room more or less the same. His room is a room
the same sum of the rooms in the same building,
the same hotel. Doors with numbers on them. I was given
a number I no longer remember. The room, the people
in the room, why the people are in the room, what will
happen after they leave the room, how what will happen
does happen and how it will change the lives of the ones
who are in the room. Sum of the room. Keys, maids,
desk clerks, cooks, maintenance. A precise number of
halls, carpets, services, the window. Sunlight. An entirely
anonymous room. We were in the room to hear John,
National Farm Director for the Central Committee of
the Party. Our Party. There is a light in the room
and the source of the light is the sun going down.
There is a lamp in the room no one has turned on. It gets
dark in the room. The rest arrive at the end of a long
drive. Several hundred miles of interstate. A stab. A blind
stab in the dark. This was John's room. This is John's
room. The size of the bed is important. It tells the cost
of the room and this must be a cheap room because
the bed is a single bed. The space is a cheap room.
This is a cheap room, one of the cheaper rooms, maybe
the cheapest room in the house.

A bed.
A chair.
A TV.
A window.
A lamp.
Doors,
keys, maids,
a desk clerk
maintenance
cooks, waiters
and waitresses.
Services.
Wandering
teeth/lips
the bed his
mouth, eyes.
Could I be other than all ear?

YOUR HONOR

could all the actions
                          Action
figures in a frieze

        a defining

                deafening

        [deafened

                        slam the tubs
explosive
irrational
dispensable

The foreman: "there's plenty more like him"

Rage
                [garble
a marvel
marbles
in your
mouth

BLAB OF THE PAVE

circumspect, shun

commend all summer long
whatever is begotten, born,

as Bride

and Pity
at my side

unrelenting
when I consider how my light is spent

delay across   amend   command

Paradise

binge

DRINKING SONG

Goya's
soggy
doggy

hard tough long fight

who declares it
who decides it
who defines it
who derides it

you must correct your course
when you take the wrong road

a child
the child
my child

glean
blare
glee

DRINKING SONGE

How does the mind move there.
"I'm your fifth cow-milker of the night"
The DJ Rocker making fun of all the calls
from farm boys producing dairy products
requesting songs. "Rock & Roll for all
you guys yankin' on cows." Twisted Sister.
Walkin' down the rocky road
down and out with so far to go
with a dull skull a hole in the hull.
Three women having a heart to heart.
What has not been heard before. A narrative
winds up on paper is not a story. Claptrap.
22 of January. Contingents marched out of
the factories. *El pueblo en armas*
guarantiza la paz digna. There is
surrender and then there is peace
with dignity. Make the Sandanistas
cry Uncle. You hit the bottle, fall
asleep.

SOUR MASH

Make me in particular particularly dead

to consign to term, tangent,

starve here in a cage

had they been capable to have understood I thought
I could have spoken of my love even to the crows
that sat upon the plowed field before me

walking the road all night tonight
walking the road all night last night
walking to road all night tonight

thus I live loveless, like a dog

had been dead
for many years

YOUR HONOR

avid
shred
flood

nothing makes sense
not leaving the University
not joining the Party
nothing makes sense
if you do not write
Poetry

nothing make sense
not leaving the University
not leaving the Party

nothing makes sense
if you do not write
Poetry

SUNDAY MORNING

The day the earth stood still

substitute fly for spider
shout for scream

                "redeem"
                a term used
                in securities

"You own the fence
you don't own the land"

Heat expands

"I'll take your coat"

pitiless
hinges

"a dirty house in a gutted world"

butterfly on a rock
random blossom
uncultivated

                harrowing

the deliberate flower

sometimes it comes
  from inside
relentless laundress

We do not make much noise

"I have my flowers outside
  in the sun"

is there somebody
somebody had

This or that
thing with wings
turned around

Think about it
what are the terms
unceasing

no longer wary
no longer wrong

This is about all that
was far before
     was for

    minute units
    footsteps
    skin on tile
      a saw

and then hung up the sign: Do not disturb
year
        voices
        instruments
        instruction

these are strict terms

the strictest terms
dictate

illiterate despair

the edge of a root
juts into space

the jut
           of it

chimes
the churchbell
in the steeple
the hour of noon

PAINT CREEK

Who was that
    what was
that was
            Thetis

then conscience forth fast
this scathe, farthing
Bear no silver over Sea

Bear no rancor
recalcitrant   truant
    rind
lethargy
Bear no

brigand   pipe   claw

clarion   frange   splay

(sporadic
spigot) put
pressure on
your tongue

VERBATIM

how much
how many
how often
how true

harvest
immediately
away   when
shoulder

standpoint
sparkle   dew
ribbon
slip   split

bow   stoop
neck
earth
admit

rider
onward
collar
wick

merry
auction
conquer
dog

chimney
greeting
rye   wool
solidly

holiday
building
borrow
baptize

mason
stars
comb
slap

sputter
crumb
medal
wheels

to bark
listen
run   marble
radio

push
eleven
leer
stern

doll
school
past four
cask (wait)

waiting
is worth
counts
bridge   jolt

incident
print
elbow
window

loyal
island
govern
corner

upheld
herald
annealed
taunt

disposed
cognition
(experience)
striving

mainspring
sculpt
the 'M'
conceals

a Methuselah
or Mrakobes

yearn
grapple
botch
mull

stigma
malinger
Beckon
askance

debacle
Recumbant
grimace
coop

assize
stringent
abjure
abrogated

The earmarks
slake
saline
despondent

indent
radiate
capillary
coast

hoarse
The pale
scruple
impart

exult
affiliation
furbish
the Fair

IV

TEDIUM RUM

He that hath the ashes of his friend

(a piece of an old boat that burnt Pompey)

But to drink of the ashes of dead relations,

all these pieces placed side by side

interminable work undertaken

by an author less hungry, less cold
than many of the poor or even workers.

Day must begin at five in the morning,
one hour a day consumed in transportation,

a North London clerk hurrying home.

The strawberry bed

offered him plump berries

from the bed.

TEDIUM GRIM

Piercing together their broken
intervals of leisure through
many years

exhausted receiver
in an immense variety of stunted
and crooked shapes

that held no station among those
who make speeches and carry on
debates

in the forest of looms

the many hundred hands in this Mill

the looms, the wheels, the hands

who turned from his own class and his own
quarter

Message in return, requiring name

and found all vanished as I had in the world

TEDIUM CRUMB

[from the advice of M. de Norpois

When I was mentioning howe dangerous
and difficult a thing it would be
to restore appropriacions, he said:

"But when all is said and done, there's
no more to it than that, and that's not
much. Nowhere does one find in his work

what one might call *movement*. His book fails
at the foundation, or rather there is no
foundation. At a time like the present,

when the ever-increasing perplexity of life
leaves one scarcely a moment for reading,
when the map of Europe is undergoing radical

alterations and is on the eve, perhaps, of
undergoing others more radical still, when
so many new and threatening problems

are arising on every side, you will allow
me to suggest that one is entitled to ask
that a poet should be something more

than a poet who lulls us into forgetting
with otiose and byzantine demonstrations
of the merits of pure form, when at any

moment we may be overwhelmed by a double
tide of barbarians, those from without
and those from within our borders."

THE BUTCHER'S THEORY
[after/for hambone bernstein

what do you know
about what I know
you don't want to

know what I do/hear
what I hear I hear
military tramp/tread

listen to the story
what do I know?
I know you're not

supposed to put all
those bright colors
and colored people

on a birthday cake.
supervisor comes in,
says "what are all

them niggers doing
on all them cakes?"
like the man says,

you give em a job
and what do you get?
a cake decorator from

Haiti. we threw them
all away. had to. The
future, necessity of

knowing it's going to
explode—not that I can't—
take the explosive I to

the farthest end/what is
going to go—any moment—
any frame anyone sees me

thru automatically behave
a measure of my abjection
this is why I am a slave

DUNCECAP

History is a flow of homogonous, linear time.

Philosophy is my self-consciousness of that fact.

Class struggle is a combat of the collective Subject.

Capitalism is the universe confined to alienation.

Communism is a state of immediate gratification.

DEAR PRUDENCE

["Whereas Marx's revolutionary teleology
contains within itself the *seeds* of a factory-
built totalitarianism," (emphasis added)
Lew Daly, *Swallowing the Scroll*, p. 71

[210]
Economism in the reverse, inevitability
of the gag, tag, *totalitarian* (if it's
inevitable then why not footnote it?)

That boy's making a case against Lenin's
State and Revolution, the occasion

transcendent freedom, going after
the whole system (supplements Schliermacher)

What if it's not a question of
what State there was, or will be,

what are the positions taken
to the State that is?

[211]
Mono
lithic development on
the basis of a single d
ream, ethics tradition
(transmystical) species
Christianity provides
what kind of base, the Cloud
of Unknowing the heir
of Economism, inevitable
and worse

[212]
Dear Lew,
so for the people
(Lukács, 'that
chaotic concept')
in that construct
to inject trans
substantiation,
the presence of
the host in the
wine and bread?

[213]
Great big brain labor!
There must be a communist way
to ground an ethics. You
would have to be able to show
—if Coard, the Escalante episode,
the murder of Commandante Ana Maria,
etc. were not related to the factory
mentality — you would have to be able
to show that — that they —
— they haven't —

[214]
" . . . they come to revolution as a discourse
and not experience."

[W.B., *Moscow Diary*, p. 56?

[215]
"Wontcha
come out
and play
yeh yeh yeh?"

DEAR MR. TROTSKY

[for Charles Bernstein

At the start of the new season whenever you like
ask the committe to interview and report as soon
as possible in a circular which carries the opposition

into the outer world, whether or not it can survive
at just how radical a level its functions are inscribed
irrespective of the number to which the youth adhere.

We will never forget the reasons for that Robespierre
transmitted by the bearers of a bureaucratic apparatus
grabbing hold, all our impetus reduced to writing

as distinct from the plausibility of intervening
given the extreme isolation at present a condition
of our profession and how few of us there really are.

RAINBOW

heavily that my love is lightly made of

cry strive as I should against them

too scholastically exprest and not with vehemency
sufficiently
                             prest

profanely laughing aloud Lord
                                    laden

                    pardon

and that to the speaking somewhat too slightly
inordinate outgoing

in pleading about things like to come and at a great
distance,

an effectual call, a personal call, a clear call
taking away,

                which makes that I cannot Expect

PEARL

flame of a circular figure & emerald

                              disproportionable

& the casual opportunity too rare
almost to make

must either be taken
emphatically, which is a fallacy,

that spumous, frothy dew or
exudation,

a festucine, pale green

& the Vulgar renders it
cum plicuisset librum
s[he shut or closed the book]

Seven times seven or 49
the Quadrant,

                    & Jubilee of thousands

DEAR JACK

maturer discernments
the brains of better heads
our whole duration
the office of our pens

there are a set of heads
prejudicate, plung'd & gravelled
they have no plea or title
the heads are carried off

this is that irradiation
which dispells pellmell
whereof common heads ought hear
who cast a careless tear

DEAR NORMA

["Is there a human voice?"
"Do we read too much?"
(overheard/hearing Cole)

Why not allow the little ones to listen to Godzilla?
Behavior,
voice barely audible
the cell, cellular

she must have been
in the place
she was not standing
Rosalind unfolds

que l'inconscient
c'est le travailleur
elle a fait le fleur
une promesse de bonheur

DEAR HILDA D.

my london

its aspect
its language
its ways of going on

my london did this london
came london her london her
part of london to london
claim london did this come
to london from london come
all

DEAR SUSAN

writ in a ring
like a runagate
yours is a banner of hope to all
I dare not call

meere dashes, strokes, *a la volée*
Antimetathesis
the smattering I have
a whisperer in corners

& she must be spared
at the blast
of his mouth
& at his bare word

PHOTOPOET

August 26. Am tired of my eyes

or are my eyes tired of looking

at something and not seeing it.

Circulation. "A woman in the street

screaming Money Money." Can you paint it?

Tonight, Barrett Watten commenting on

the totemic or hyperreal, a 20 dollar bill

in a Russian movie. Only the effect.

The wastes. Real doubts.

THE REAL THING

Spicer's want/wanting
"But what you *want* to say—the business of wanting
comes from the outside, like it wants five dollars
being ten—that kind of want is the kind of thing
which is the real thing—the thing you didn't want
to say in terms of your own ego—in terms of your
image, in terms of your life, in terms of everything

"I get up books for the shops," he said

Dispatch, this knave's tongue begins to double

My shame will not be shifted with my sheet

"Stop," said the King

                                shrink, shrank, shrunk

flow of foul mouth

CASSAMASSIMA

[after reading *Into Distances*

And this Queen rode undisputed mistress of a green
glassy sea, some of whose waves were breaking over
her bow in a wild way, I can tell you, and I used to

be giving her up for lost and foundered every page,
till I grew older, and perceived that she was not
in the slightest danger in the world. A good deal of

dust, and fuzzy stuff like down, had in the course
of many years worked through the joints of the case,
in which the ship was kept, so as to cover all the sea

with a light dash of white, which if anything improved
the general effect, for it looked like the foam and froth
raised by the terrible gale the good Queen was battling

against. So much for *La Reine*. We have her yet
in the house, but many of her glass spars and ropes
are now sadly shattered and broken,—but I will not

have her mended; and her figure-head, a gallant warrior
in a cocked-hat, lies pitching head-foremost down
into the trough of a calamitous sea under the bows—

MOUTH/PIECE

[for Eliot Weinberger

Perfunctory blur the unbroken
stimulation and expediency of expression
in Langland's lines,

what kynne I come of,

the plowshare, horseshoe, a half-penny candle

all well called away,

commination (threat of wrath)

unsitting (unfitting)

javel (low class rascal)

---

35. C. Brooke-Rose, "Ezra Pound: Piers Plowman in the Modern
Waste Land" in *A Review of English Literature*, II, April 1961, p. 77.

TEMPERED BROGUE

I stole the book. Jane's

Lydia. She's a riot.

Gothic? Floors and doors groan under the body
passing through them.

The return to routine limitations.

Dances when discouraged now

or as a relief from the bks.

SLUCTE

Both she & they   excluded

in Right of Representation [from the Father
                                    [from the State

affliction like a dimension may be divided

a more powerfull specificall unions

fictions of what should be (not histories)

& indissoluble Sympathy to all

CHAFFARE

Rolling recriminations

Moral Coherence anulling all

a clear declaration of doctrine

But Truth would not have it so,

for she is a bastard. Her father

is falsehood, displaying

in full the enormous driving force we call

Capital

JACK ATTACK

you said it about the kids on the bus. the bind we're in.
if and when. we have been taught how not to write.
they strip you of that. and you will never know what
it is. you said it about the kids on the bus. our price.

what is happening in a 70 mile radius. the comment
that Jack made. decide what you want to do and do it
and see what happens next. organized from the outside in.
a simple thing. I wish we could sit down and discuss it.

for the first time in forty years, feeling the truth, living
the truth. we have lived a lie. the lie, its scope and scale.
your children will live better. they force us to accept
their conditions. we are from another world. bad on

the blood of the rest of the world. what happens when you
have a bloodsucker. it turns on its own. the reality of what
your life is really like. everything must be relearned. history
makes you strong. we are coming out of the land of Oz.

MIGHTY ONE

the world
for song-ok

Max was bright and pretty good at
getting in and out of trouble but
he'd never forgot the day he broke
his Mom's mysterious old statue
and found the Cosmic Cap inside.

How was he to know it made him
the "Mighty One" able to travel
instantly from place to place by
means of time portals? And how
were Max, his Cosmic Cap, and his

two friends and protectors, wise?

THE OPENING GUNS OF WORLD WAR III

[Notes from a lecture by Mac Warren:
Labor at the Crossroads
Minneapolis, Minnesota, 1/21/91

The case: we face a social crisis.
Summary of the decisive points.
Demoralization. Demobilization.
Oct. 1987 stock market crash. 1934.

Tremendous defeats, important fights.
Three big battles. San Francisco
longshoremen. Minneapolis teamsters.
Toledo Auto-Lite. Birth of the CIO.

Political movement. Social movement.
Roosevelt given credit for giving us
everything we took. The giant baby steps
that need to be taken towards changing

everything. A deep and important lesson:
You do not vote for bourgeois politicians.
The ocean of blood they call World War II.
Postwar relative prosperity in the developed

countries. Coming out the bloodbath the world
had a different face. Coming out of the slaughter
pen the explosion of the Colonial Revolution.
Part of the deal: driving working people out

of politics. The Witch Hunt was aimed at
the political layers of the working class.
We stand on the threshold of a new crisis.
Oil. Nixon wage-freeze speech. Recession.

The world is different today. Germany
and Japan bolstered U.S. dollars during
the crash. Malcolm X: U.S. Imperialism
is the last great empire. THEY HAVE NO

NEW MARKETS THEY HAVE NO WHERE
TO GO NO WHERE TO EXPAND THEY
HAVE NO PERSPECTIVE FOR MOVING
FORWARD IN THE CONTEXT OF MOVING

FORWARD IN THE CONTEXT OF THIS
CRISIS. Malcolm X: Uncle Sam will never
win another war. Let's open the floor
for discussion. Nan, were you going

BRAIN LABOR

[notes from Pat Grogan's lecture
"Woman & Socialism"/Des Moines

What is necessary to reproduce the next generation

the value of women's labor power, we lower the labor
power
          based on the sheer abuse

comparable worth has nothing to do with how labor
power
is determined

what you think you're worth compared to what others
think your worth

without understanding
the law of surplus labor

there is no such thing
as the 'family' in the abstract

exploited workers—lower wages
          lower labor power

women also decide
must overcome

The lesson from backward attitudes
of male workers
all oppressed people

The standard of Beauty
a terrific suffering

Have you ever seen a picture of a picket-line?
South Africans, strikers, their fists in the air
the surrounding spatial environment
their outward extension into space
a real contribution to consciousness
try to distinguish an individual face
impossible. Women do not devalue human life
they assert the value of their own life
and that is a radical statement in this
society

anarchy
the fact
of being
female

children
everything
we have
to give

We are not animals
we have gone way beyond
the fate of being female

non-union labor lowering
the value of labor power

we are in a system
it runs on human waste

the standard of living
a relative measure
counter-relief

for the day when every
laborer is valued

concentration
not on the object

documentary accuracy
open on Sunday

we will depict
the present day

childbearing

the cops and the capitalist
courts

he was a truckdriver
she was a waitress
(heaven forbid) the scum
of the earth

and their child
was Baby M

["the sperm of William Stern"

We bear the children
We bear the lion's share

the view of the child
when the child exists
to satisfy the cravings
of adults

society has no need
to see bloodlines
perpetuated

involuntary
servitude

a contract to
deliver

                sold

a child

subhuman
subservient
substitute
substandard
substance
substantiate
submarine

a cry of mutual recognition

declared in a catalogue

where the real body of life

is made

the struggle for access to art

something we are going to

have to come to grips with

reticulate

and can
latitude

allowable
adhesion

retained
occurrence

narrower
partition

barring
perimeter

spirals
slip the

softer
thwarting?

workers concept theater

kill, cut & sausage

a killfloor steward in Iowa

"We never really had much representation"

"We knew we had an enemy, and the cops
were not our friends"

they smash you
they arrest you
they beat you up

You got an idea?
Bring it in here.

The prejudices, the oppression, the differences
that divide us

the practice and process of active solidarity

marsellaise

volumes in the voice of
london—severities

I was only a working man
a heavy foot on the stairs

circumstances did not allow
plaster to be taken for stone

extracts from a letter
a shop with a room behind it

and cellar below
Sunday a quiet restful day

unmarked/unencouraged
stood by the side of those

selma

Let others bear the title of a novel or poem.

One tack to take towards an anticipation of what I would
call a plural writing,

to excavate from her discursiveness and even more
startling work,

and concede nothing to the "human" that society
is always ready to appeal to as an alibi for the *subhuman,*

"English is not our language," argued Takiyah Hudson,
17, a high school senior who lives in Harlem.

"Our language has more rhythmic tones."

drunken/driving song

lapped
in a wave,

rope
flopped
dully,

as in
the "old"
days

toad's list of things to do

A few notes on Langland.
Must "see it feelingly."
Need to read Chaucer and
Milton, not to mention
Gower, Spenser, Sidney,
Dante—the list is long.
The tremor of the future
in the reproducing Past.
A poem close to its class.
Hopkins heard its English.
All time happens now.
This is a lesson from
the work of Susan Howe.

WITCH HUNT

"She has taught us historical passion"
[from the Communist Party Historian
Group's Tribute to Dona Torr

then said the Interpreter
he went clothed in garments such as they
now even every one of those things also
where he was now got hard by the hill

the cellar door of the mansion
he would come to the house of the
Interpreter
was walking in the fields

was reading in a book
where we shall receive instruction
and Garments that will make us shine like the sun
City of Destruction

Liar alone was led to her
begging her blessing
advocates of the arches
as high as trees

calves, sheep, heifers and rams
birds and herbs, the blood of lambs
the East and the Sun
allusion now lost

site of a shrine
sought clothes
accompanying dignity
the king is the cat

a popular song
"how may I save my soul"
only one argument
in the poem

To provide for a passage out of America.
What I remember is the narration of the last
day (events conspire, by accident) making the ghost
walk again and bringing Benjamin into the Wilderness
with Hutchinson accomplishing in imagination
—the imagination of the concept—(an imaginary concept)
what the accidental character of events conspired to
prevent: Benjamin's transposition onto American space
[the cabaret song in *Moscow Diary* also the Klondike,
the equation of Russia c. 1926-7 with the Klondike]
Asja Lacsis singing 'San Francisco.' The irony
the effect of the Institute's removal to NY
was to change—"soften"—the terms. Historical
materialism becomes Critical Theory. But you
were not putting Benjamin in Central Park
you were putting him in New England
—transpotion/'dialectical image.' Benjamin
with Anne Hutchinson's face. Susan Gevirtz:
"Hutchinson doesn't have a face."

Resting unrest
pressing ashen
pale breast
Roman waste
or purely theoretical anarchist
went me to london
under the wing
The intellectuals the work attracted were mostly literary
personalities with a sentimental rather than scientific
relation to the tradition of Trotsky's ideas. Sympathies
to surrealism. Fourier: *Thèorie des quatre mouvements*
(Marx defended Fourier to Grün). Technology
and its sobriety. *Eikon Basilike:* that the true thing
determines itself only through the false thing, through
that which makes itself falsely known. What may not be
chronologically true may carry a further, more figurative
charge. Hart Crane was murdered in 1932.
Der Anfang [The Beginning]

Asja Lacsis (remembering a conversation with Benjamin): "He expressly emphasized that in his work he described Baroque plays in search of linguistic form as a phenomenon analogous to Expressionism."

Susan Buck-Morss (p. 49): "Benjamin's original conception, a politicized version of Sleeping Beauty as a fairy tale of 'awakening' retold along Marxist lines, was intended to "set free the huge powers of history asleep within the 'once upon a time' of classical historical narration."

Susan Buck-Morss (p.35): "As storyteller, Benjamin seems to be in complicity with children—and also with the lower classes for whom education has traditionally been a lesson in intellectual humiliation."

(There was an essay for community

college, my first now lost.

The theme, my first job.

SiouxPreme Packing Plant,

Sioux City, Iowa. Received

a "C" he accused me of copying

Upton Sinclair).

eisenhower jacket

"The critic is
similarly under
no obligations
to sociological
values, as the
social conditions
favorable to the
production of
great art are not
necessarily those
at which the social
sciences aim."
Northrop
Frye/1955)

th eincomplete

strategies of the paratactic work

placement, one thing after another

spatial or temporal both structure as sequence

epitome of counter-narrative, arrests narrative

read through

        patrimony and patriotism

Prometheus

unbound.

melancholy molly

the last copyist to understand
lightnings render reddest strain
repeated simultaneous sound
we are still standing in the same place

Marx: "homologous potatoes"
much as potatoes in a sack
form a sack of potatoes
She is making a hoard of the holy men in hell

not for no other now no longer
my learning no bitterer bid
and will not stop at exposition
all tis false theatrical

heavy paragraphs of exact statement
a room in which we are fully awake
alert to each exigency/a farm room
pallid pillars of painted wood

the raft's soft sailcloth
arbitrary permeable barriers
old family furniture its past
he said it was just as well

she could never remember
have had enough of daylight
metal filing cabinets and shelves
elongated frames of the same

orange infant face. maroon ground.
brown boat on a lake. mountains/fog.
walked once to the left
then back again while talking

back to the one that caught my eye
a social realist portrait
firm vertical line marking
the mangled body's shoulder length hair

the hair a blur that disperses
the sharp yellow red of the shawl
she had on. put the lenin back
you wrote as day broke

and pushed him through
ralph's window as a joke
the names that fall
are fruit from the tree

though the fruit of
the love be bruised
she describes how the mind
with restless pleasure

adheres he retells the tale
as it ought to have been
not what it was
as a further clause

added to the margins
of an original document
hunger and the writing
that promises nothing

merrytown assembly

her blue striped cotton dress
all clean and always washed
she went away to work in a factory
rough and harsh to see

anna and her mother made
ready for the wedding day and night
sally who was in her trances
she could not sleep much in the night

her pen hastily lifted
and she hated the house
and all the work in it
does he not ride before

his mother seeking his mother?
a woman becomes a great name
what chance does she have
Isis in search of Osiris

a woman entangled
out of the open glow
abject
          she broke

there is only one cry
recorded she is in a flow
of talk and we must not
interrupt

if to the pain of great
privation alliteration
as a locking
[device]

associative immersion
nominally free
hostility to a hard lord
periods of high mortality

dialectical rhythms
   [12/19 for Mary Shelley
   for the gift of flying

Karl and Mary as coauthors
my drive to structure/her
correspondence. Mary's is not
a neutral voice she is recounting

what happened/my interpretation
rests on the reconstruction
of what has passed between us
"You know I am Dora" Dora

the desire to live
the instinctive is in the unconscious
spontaneous unleashed
the insult a blow so severe

the insult I could never remember.
we are building a house in the space of
a few hours, a few days!
we have no history. have no home.

make him understand his position
the problem with what I am
that was last night/justified
like a mother in her child.

on the way to buffalo

at this point of exhaustion
the thought occurs in the chatter
constructed by what forces
you have no control of this

poised yet lost in traffic
lost or is it that or not
I don't know her now I knew her
when rumors were only rumors

conversation in the galley
about a vertical liftoff
none have experienced it before
you take off and go straight up

register invitation in the remark
from a traveller with nowhere to go
"I was just wondering
if we had time for another drink"

at stake the shaping
of agency and more
floating in a cask.
ground speed. altitude.

this would be to ask for
everything chronology
long standing grievances
impossibility of naming

let the moral aspect
fall by the way
it is what happened
commingle

langland left off

polemical stiffening
linguistic hegemony
M. de Clèves got sick and died
he remembered going

in a submarine and being
disappointed by the ride
"you wait and you wait and you wait for it
then all you do is go down

and back up." they fill the water
up the tubes. water deposits.
testicles bloated up. a doctor
wrote him a note: "good luck"

a boat was arriving
out of the open glow
the doctrine latrine
shipped/took shape

all trading done
the 10th congress/early '21
what do you want
a blessing?

lipara
          [for Susan Howe

This onely is a Worke too

That it were a new & no
                    authentick

Works have an age
they have a stint
& period

meer English
& English pens
acknowledging

the frown of Theology

& leading part
of learning

Who was the author of those few fair minutes?

It were not
a wary or
evasive
method

to be able
immediately
to offer
such apt

concernment
the tender
taking up

perpetual

impairment

The question might be made
of inconsiderate
misconstruction

deception
& miscarriage

above the eye
in distillations
without one drop

a fugitive faith
that from the name
descend to the bare

term of Prophet
confederating

Ours is the ordinary
& open way

doublings & wrenches

given occasion
by a doubtful work

these little citizens

like an excellent Artist
alters or
perverts

nor disdain to suck Divinity

she only is

There is
therefore
no deformity

Champion!

I am in great care
& fares for you

adorned with Typographie
expatiate & farre

arreareges
to credit what our eyes

rise into Similitude

expect impossibilities
that Poetic knack

fanatical integritie
in the vaporous State

What great charges
we ar now att

One common conversation
one common name
common to us all

& duly sounding
begat the doubt

Tinsell
the draughts of
Consulary date

whether the Opaline
cast off

will it consist
with either
But other

Some affectionate
friend

HOMAGE TO MARY ENGLE

a penny to keep the Secret

what first induced me to Rhyme

The mother would often stop the wheel

while the laboring classes remain as blind

drudging at home year after year

a barley loaf or dish of potatoes

a husband or something like that name
I have wiped out,

others I corrected 20 times over
till their original form was entirely
lost as the Morning Walk now extant

and that is not my own

The rusticity of the alliterative school

The practical art of the chant

Never to be able to theorize

who must therefore turn books to our own account

quickened to write. Rhyme

has its origins in vernacular Latin

The waste of hours that make our day

There is waste in what we say

Never alone in a room without walls

every fragment of time

devoted to the Nine

inclined into Rhythm

precedents of audacity

some bastard piece of fortitude

contingent inequality

calcin'd, as not to miscall

infirmities, in the large Expression

rending neerer, & draw

powerfullest arms

a cup of cold water

untractable obstacle

marshalling all

Young Headlong Racket to the last akin

That edens self in freedoms infant sphere

Must bear being noticed by his proper name

And link the weapons of his broken speech

And hurl bad english and a stop marks time

Stanzas to Cobbets truth and Comic Rhymes

Whose blasts blow blessings every time they blow

As condemned transports on the way to hell

The half thatched mouldering hovels of distress

Their rage and given his utmost fury vent

Who might as well write letters to the dead

Trifling and such art thou rare pararrell

Two years before the mast

It all comes back to me now

What does it mean to make literary

The grass in the pasture is rudimentary

The act of writing physical unsettling

increment of isolation and vulnerability

I wasn't even aware that I was writing poetry

Now I know what they mean by a sacred cow

Something in a discourse that cannot be stated

If you see God's face

you are incinerated

Now I know that it softens

when you no farther may

that before was ground of all

that all this world, that bore a child

We meet so seldom by tree or stone

Extant possessor, speak terror

toward at that time usurpers none

There will never another deprive improvement

for now your speech to me is clear

kindly consolation, you have been both

But now I am here in your presence

Start with a statement and move on after it as indicated, there would have to be and was—there was, what was there—what's the matter? Allot. Not a jot. Impatient though, as any Joe. He said the line speed had gotten vicious and the grievance procedure was skewed. Endowed by a violet impetus, the rhythm of the plot as it develops. "Revival" was a word that Marx wrote down, then crossed out in the draft of a letter to Vera Zasulich. When I think of her now I don't see her I hear her and I don't hear her speaking to me. But you can't just study these signposts one by one like points on a compass to which you continually turn and return to refer. Work you postpone and would better avoid. Vallejo and Ponge with an eye on Brecht. Thought of József. Began the night with four poems by Zukofsky. Every day now. Beside the barn beyond the fence a mile before the house the road toward town the sound of a car but no car passed. He could hear the road, the night, where the road curved on and away, beyond the barn beside the fence a mile below the hill. Here is not a third part of the history of The Hundred Years War.

This is the last time and coughing up peony Penny my
cousin's name embarrassed for her husband, resolute or
dissolute did he think hard or think at all, everything
returns to the chord in accord or discord discovery
recovery covey cull the hull of the boat below the stern
bow birds brave the bilge who can hear them huddled
in a corner brighten the corner where you are humble pie
by Rumplestiltskin why did I cry tonight, and then
arranged the books in reading not alphabetical order
an entirely subjective method not to be duplicated in any
archive except yours, dear, turn the page, this is the page,
the book, bereft of a binding, tossed casually on the shelf
along with the rest arranged that no one will read who
reads to purely pass the time, it helps to arrange to have
something to do in order to think, begin thinking, that's
what I was thinking, throw the novels all away, they take
up too much space, your story had better not be taken
out, so that it became imperative, to judge from the dust
on the ledges and I could not breathe, coughed, coughed
hard and often and coughed up the years as you
compiled and refused to be catalogued.

The shout from the audience in The Castro, "So die!"
at the Sartrean mother, and the laughter following.
That sounds like Jack. What do Marx & Mary Engels
have to say about Zola Balzac Stendhal, the bolts of
culture still unbroken before the night of broken glass.
In the Eisenhower version of the domestic system, when
writing is half-forgotten, given if it is given at all and is
something that can be taken away, how easy to overlook
the need to make a categorical leap, a call to arms for
the emerging class, an address to the ruined artisans
in the second generation of manualists. I am sitting here
now alone writing under the shadow of the Society of
December 10 the scandalous reciprocity you absolutely
knew, that it was *this* and *this* and *this* which coalesce
immediately in a measure of the only hope we have,
the drag of rhythm and the best possible pleasure we can
possibly imagine, our child the praxis in a constellation
of concern. What do I do for a living? There are many
others more deserving who undergo elimination holding
glimmerings into the kind of ingenuity at the confines of
my wish to reproduce your world without disturbing it.
Tone is the tuning fork. The shoemaker makes the entire
shoe. A happy ending is a form of gratitude.

Who can I turn to for the gift of your coming into my
heart, that I might tell the loneliness of lyric expression
at the end of the 20th century? To be conscious of
the capacity you must feel, whose accent, for the hour,
lives in my ears. You would have found me finical,
bending a pen to the thin partition, as proud of a penny
as a pound of gold, squandering my meager resources
receding like the glow of opinion the wide lake dark
and high. A private letter is the logical beginning of
every day fused into the pure appearance of narration.
Hunt's leading article in *The Examiner*, 12 October, 1817,
"Fellow Creatures Suffered to Die in the Streets."
I have been to work in a garden, a voluntary society
of free and equal human beings, and I would propose
that communism is not a philosophy, but a body —
a physiology — the permanent demand for the Promise
of Happiness — the Dutchess of Dunghill — a field hand
with a hoe and she is coming into view. Who am I to
tremble in the path of her advancing? A shelf has been
made by blasting rock to form the road — a knot of light
— a sunrise out of a sea of blood —
some secret of the fields.

THE MORNING WALK

blackthorn bower I often pulld my hat over my eyes to watch the rising of the lark or to see the hawk hang in the summer sky & the kite take its circles round the wood I often lingered a minute on the woodland stile to hear the woodpigeons clapping their wings among the dark oaks I hunted curious flowers in rapture & muttered thoughts in their praise I lovd the pasture with its rushes & thistles & sheep tracks I adored the wild marshy fen with its solitary hernshaw sweeing along in its mellancholy sky I wandered the heath in raptures among the rabbit burrows & golden blossomd furze I dropt down on the thymy molehill or mossy eminence to survey the summer landscape as full of rapture as now I markd the varied colors in flat spreading fields checkerd with closes of different tinted grain like the colors in a map the copper tinted colors of clover in blossom the sun-tannd green of the ripening hay the lighter hues of wheat & barley intermixd with the sunny glare of the yellow carlock & the sunset imitation of the scarlet headaches with the blue cornbottles crowding their splendid colors in large sheets over the land & troubling the cornfields with destroying beauty the different greens of the woodland trees the dark oak the paler ash the mellow lime the white poplar peeping above the rest like leafy steeples the grey willow shining chilly in the sun as if the morning mist still lingered on its cool green I felt the beauty of these with eager delight the gadflys noonday hum the fainter murmur of the beefly 'spinning in the evening ray' the dragonflys in spangled coats darting like winged arrows down the thin stream the swallow darting through its one archd brig the shepherd hiding from the thunder shower in a hollow dotterel the wild geese skudding along & making all the letters of the alphabet as they flew the motley clouds the whispering wind that muttered to the leaves & summer grasses as it flitted among them like things at play I observd all this with the same raptures as I have done since but I knew nothing of poetry it was felt & not utterd Most of my sundays was spent in this manner about the fields

John Clare

I

History as a continuum of collapses.
Histor is in origin the eyewitness, the one who has
seen.
　　　Or: "an experience of history as what is
already there without ever appearing before our eyes"

Alastor, the wanderer, the spectre of the unburied

"An archive document [...] draws its value from its
place in a chronology and a relationship of proximity
and legality with the past event."

Marx: *Gattungswesen* (species-being) against cycle
and continuum. *Ereignis* (event). The event conceived
no longer as spatio-temporal determination but as
the opening of the primary dimension where all spatio-
temporal dimensions are based.

A perfect pleasure outside
any measurable dimension.

9/17

the available keys

eliminare: a poetic word, mostly early and late Latin
possessio: in the sense of 'estate'
sternitur: "throw down" *sternere* is mostly
　　　　　Poetic and not found in Prose
　　　　　before the Augustan period

"By imagining the lived experience of actors
in particular oppositional moments ... "

what linguistics has made part of our
responsibility,

all exiles or figures of displacement, lies
in the 'bastard' nature of their thought

Caillard, his claim to author his own work

suffers not only damage besides one who has fallen
into unhappiness

Sudden onset of sleep
such as falls on those who have wept

which in the process of assimilation
in Northern and Western dialects of this period
would become t
                                severe phonetic spellings

marked or made
and if it is really as early as the end
or formal term of address within the family

[which] here becomes the linking-word of the group of
five stanzas which follow, and thus the word has to
be used ten times in the positions fixed by the form

in working the word into these positions the poet
sometimes strains the meaning as when the recognized
'sense limit' is extended—

EXTEND THIS IDEA TO THE GOWER GLOSSARY
(each repeated word as a linking-word)

Working the same word into multiple positions

" ... simultaneous perceptions of events
passing by quickly, too quickly, and of each
hour and minute being entirely lived or made
use of, saturated time."

(Poets themselves accept their own uninterrupted
transformation)

The hand that holds the pen

"Emancipation, in Roman and civil law, means to be
freed from control; from the Latin *mancipare*, to seize
with the hand (*manus*); emancipation, literally to be
unhanded"

"Writing is an activity of the hand as much as is
plowing: the importance lies in the relation of
the hand to a tool, even if the tool is as slight
as a pen ... "

the tools, the pens, the plows
the language
the work that must be done

11/28 (Dusk)

To dream of including everything is to dream of being
included. And then intention sidles in dispersing
force. An allegory, not elegy. This will be my life
work. Have had presentiments all day. It will include
everything: lyric, song, rhyme, narrative & commentary
& stage (theater), translations, adaptations, assimilations
—appropriated. A compendium and vision of Historical
Materialism. The Promise of Happiness.

I am caught in a conversation.
I am 37 this March. Conversations with Eckermann.

Holy Church is Hope. The foundation of all future work.
The intention here is to base myself. Brace myself.

There is no more
There must be no more
America

          This is when I can think, when the lamp comes
on and casts shadows on stacks of books. The struggle
with thought. There is no struggle at dusk. Peace. Or
prospects. Looking forward, anticipatory, not projection.
The feeling for a future. It is clear by now that all my life
I have had absolutely no interest in my life, circumstances
an accident which I must exploit. The only deliberation
has been my reading. This is the grace of the book,
and here I make an absolute distinction between the life
and the book. My life is my book. The rest is prone,
addicted, overcome. "I have never been here."

The way home

in the brief space
of 340 pages as well as the political and family
life of the ancient world and the
Middle Ages

　　　　　that this book is a
　　　　　"conspectus"

some of the author's terse notes

notes are not a
shortcoming

else whose book would not attain
　immeasurable dimensions

DANCE THEATER OF PINA BAUSCH

A vast square room, all in white. The rear wall is
composed entirely of glass, large squares of glass.
To the left is a spacious desk and an arm chair of
austere design. A smaller desk is to the right.
　Faint bursts of music come and go.
　A clerk is at the smaller desk.
　It is still only a tinge.
　What color?
　A light rose.

"[N]ote that the imaginations of the mind (the passions of the mind) regarded in themselves, contain no error (or that the mind does not err from that which it imagines, but only insofar as it is considered as wanting the idea which acts off the existence of those things which it imagines as present to itself ...[which is to say that the mind errs to the extent that it is unfree to imagine] 'For if the mind while it imagined things not existing as present to itself knew at the same time that those things did not in truth exist, we must attribute this power of imagination to an advantage of its nature and not a defect, that is...if the mind's faculty of imagining be free'...free, i.e., 'That thing is said to be FREE which exists by the mere necessity of its own nature and is determined in its actions by itself alone.'

[This means I am free to write about the Party as an imagined body/politic not simply as an 'experience' that writing which would adhere to the 'experience' only in the form of a memoir or travel narrative or document errs on the side of truth—that the truth is not in the literal accounting but the imagination of that body the dream of that militant, social body].

But the important thing is to mythologize it. This will be a chronicle of the Society. How was it organized. It is not a group that exists. What is its relation to Sport? The stadium, the library. The Society was a fragmentary component within the embracing structure of the School. The School did not exist in isolation. The concern of the present chronicle is to reconstruct the process by which an idea was conceived, developed, and evolved to endanger the structure of the School itself. The degeneration of an idea, from fact to fantasy. Did it just endanger the School, or does it do away with the School altogether? What happens to the School after the fiasco of this idea? The scandal? It is forced to defend itself, to justify itself. It must turn on the members of the Society, and punish them. Expulsion? Summary execution? Too easy, too ready a solution. Court cases. The record is in the court cases. Everything that needs to be known. Start looking up summaries. Previous authorities. Authority for what argument. That you are looking for legal justification for a form of martial law. The extant records, evidence. The Easter Bunny debate, the Mary Engle archive, the Rapist-Communist. What was the other one.

Not long ago it seemed unthinkable. A movement long since past. As if it still existed and were standing in the way. It does not belong to the present. *Menschheitsdammerung* published in 1920 work by Trakl, Lasker-Schüler, Heym and Stadler. A pre-condition. Emotive, rhetorical, declamatory (Lukács) "caught up in the kicks and blows." Social Realism, its demonstrable antithesis. A third-hand classicism, junk clumsily glued. In the emotional outbursts in the art of that period, archaic-utopian hypostases. The poets had no object outside themselves. Two minuses produce a plus. Passions of an earlier period still stir. The part of the artist to shatter every image of the world. Christ's scourge driving the money changers from the temple. It suffered far more from a neglect of form, a plethora of expression crudely put. A grasp undeformed by education. Else-Lasker Schüler. Czech, Latvian and Yugoslav artists about 1918. Expressionism has not yet ceased to exist. We traded our painted glass for a print of it. We have not even begun to consider it.

The relation of Thetis to Achilles. The *Iliad* makes explicit, emphatic use of her as mother—a kourotrophos—and protector, i.e., this aspect of Thetis, her maternal, protective power—also her role in the theogonic myth of succession. Thetis initially appears as a figure of destitution. Helplessness and grief. Female deities notable in Greek and Indic mythologies to the prototype of an Indo-European goddess, Ausos. Asia is either the literal end of life or destiny, the index of whether one's actions are appropriate to one's nature. "Thetis and her mythology are put to radically different use in the *Iliad*. Through her the *Iliad* offers not the immortality of the Aethipis but a conception of heroic stature as inseparable from human limitation and of heroic experience as a metaphor for the condition of mortality." Thetis' overwhelming potential as *Isthmian 8* reveals (Pindar). It lies at the heart of Aeschylus' *Prometheus Bound*. Thetis: "an inconsolable mother, unable to save her only child."

Ellen's refusal to allow the contempt of the younger women for women who were mothers go unargued. Her stand against contempt, and for some sense of a biological bond. Something that passes between the mother and her child that inheres, irreducible. Open to reactionary interpretation, it still must be recognized and defended. The assault on proletarian women double-edged. They must be kept as an integral— because low-paid—component in the workforce, but their labor cannot be an act of freedom. They must work in unfreedom, bound to the home. Men must be made to share in the work transpiring there: Reproduction.

Mary's letters. The Mother and the Party then coexist as twin sources of instruction that indicate vocation, vertue, the hope of a higher good in the Book—literature that has suffered the institutions of learning, which can no longer be seriously considered as a repository of truth except to the extent that it can be pillaged. But that my books might one day be found among a catalogue of Party literature, or on a sales table—the negotiation it took to set up a table, to sell the Paper and related books. The explosiveness of that literature. And it is useful. The primary fact. What makes 'Party' literature. What distinguishes it from all other written work is is usefulness. Applicability to current questions in debate. The Baby M case, Baby M.

II

Newly arrived
why shouldn't I look
he said, into the distance as I walk?

The permanent inscription above the door

The cold touch of Marxist thought

It is real and great and does not extract
the true poetic correlate. Engels once called it
the "dream of a thing" in the world

          surplus of tendency and latency

the more distinctly and it does not envy

The communist poet
open and active, open to change
literature could readily drown

as if there was no subjective factor

Once one chooses to accept Marxism
countless problems of motion and incompleteness

Mountains turn around
                        forming-transforming

It is this imagination, dialectically trained and
mediated

When the imagination will no longer be the social
outcast

It shows itself most clearly in dramatic form
The determining instance of social class

What is added to the subject while it is still being driven
away
            The world wants to be changed

The history of communism, a storehouse

almost undiscovered—despite the Faust
material, or Prometheus

A new kind of historical poetry the petit-bourgoisie
did not want and could not have

There is a kind of nature to which no response has been
given since Rimbaud

Too manifest a state of insobriety

a certain amount of stimulant had been permitted
along the way

the least articulate, the London poor

her earnings at an artificial flower factory

It was a short street
like many in London
degenerating

That from no point can anything
like a general view of its totality
be obtained

where oratory was to be heard and debate was open

his brief, stammering protests against this or that
social wrong

"We are the lower orders, we are the working classes"
he said bitterly to his friend, and that seemed the
final answer to all his aspirations

But I who am at home who do not walk out I could
write to you all day

Mac, who found it necessary to say,
despite the femininity of his nerves,
his excitement, that there was no 'heart'
in it,

But that there is heart in it, that is why
I am writing. That there is the full—
             to confer the full measure
of Love to the desire to do away with all forms
of property.

The months, the weeks, the hours of that year.

Wit, hilarity and observation were mingled
in their conversation.

Rendering every sentence a flash of light.

When the only possible experience
is boredom, lies,
                    everyday life
in any city suffice

(Benjamin) 'the poverty of experience'

Out of this poverty concentrate
on the Book—the Imaginary—authority

whose claim to legitimation once
was experience

> to take note

(having no wish to
experience it pre-
ferring that the
camera should)

The instrumentally manipulated or dominated

then, "I will never have my signature
on a body of work that exists as an
alienated or detached object"

The native infirmity of the worker

whose space is governed

as written in various hands on sheets of different sizes
made with the object of recording all the material upon
which money could be raised to meet the needs of the State
and the
ministers
ornaments
"pix" a case of silver which bare the sacrament.

'The Heart' was Hart Crane's cherished nickname

"His roots in the depression" [?]

Nyerges collapses beginning and end

The fascination in gross misreading

Benjamin's astonishment at the ignorance
of a Moscow intellectual who insisted
that Shakespeare wrote before the
invention of printing

Hart Crane was murdered in 1932

What may be chronologically true

What may not be chronologically true
can carry a further, more figurative
charge
        trembling (*Schaudern*)
plumpes denken (crude thinking)
emotion (*Ruhrung*) Bloch's title
Spuren (traces, tracks)

What is writing. Empty promises. Are we?

Things got pretty bad in the back room.

Patches of voices. You ever watch a bricklayer
pick up a pencil?

To make a diagram, how
is that instrument held.

What is she writing
and for whom?

It was a surprise to know anybody who had seen them
    and that they had a name

There were two addresses, a town and a country
    one written a long time ago in ink

and the London light screened by the high opposing
houses

It was impossible to fit into that.

I am no longer that person.

There was something in music
when one played alone, without
thoughts. It was the price.
It stung and tried her.
The grouping would not recur.

The tea was made in a jug
echoing tread.

It would be unjust to herself
to share.

She was not conscious, in smiling, of the expression
on her face.

Her sphere, to this
she had attained.

She bore her degradation
no longer the consequence
of her own volition.

She began to copy something
using the pen with difficulty
and taking extreme pains.

Thank you for coming
There is no one and you

invite to the address
this talk, are welcome

This is a talk about a book

The bitter social fact
of its existence

We rise and rivet
stigma, insulation
and prepared for it

forging and foraging
will not produce or
transport

what goes on

Dear Ellen,

the baby's happy
when your back's

to the wall. "Speak,
and step forward."

I am a migrant.
Immense potential.

I went to the town
meeting with you.

We talked about
the threat, and how

they have no help.
Hormel in Ottumwa

is closing in August.

III

What true responsibility might be
his 'clerkly' vocation
a serious (religious)
writer waiting in hope
for "words of grace"

during the millenium after the fall of the
Western Empire (5th Century AD)
its missionary impulse
the Materialist
propound to bold

ends honor, ingots
or war
now hard, and harsher
purge for her
repletion

(al-ya'ibu, the one who is absent,
as in the Arab grammarians

(mu, which indicates the moaning
sound when the mouth is closed

The Western unvoicing

(must measure the depth of oppression
by the intensity of the loss

what has been lost

the most heroic of sacrifices
are capable of being made
under the auspices of the
simplest words

depositories
of the Records
where the work is
continuing, task

of turning
into English
newer methods
of unearthing

See what were
the roads where
a way is wanting
has never ceased widening

an event

that imaginary

magnet

locality (Celan)

a tattered flag

whose library was eight inches by four

one could page me

chummying

Brecht

Pummel,

wherein he

is said to

have carried

something

"To follow one's own conviction is certainly more than to
give oneself over to authority; but by the conversion of
opinion held on authority into opinion held out of personal
conviction, the content of what is held is not necessarily
altered, and truth does not necessarily take the place
of error."

That
cannot be studied
carelessly, mir nichts dir nichts

Books as often remarkable for their
facility as by their amazing
emptiness

a noticeable gap in the absence of
a paragraph

Not only Ricardo but Marx
as well affirms the general
tendency of rent to rapidly
increase under all and any
circumstances (rent may even
increase when the price of
grain is steady or even
decreasing)

the pré

the trace

authorial self-consciousness
as old as the Book itself

It is not a question of whether or not

not even a question of figuring

vast wastes of time
squandered

experience
without theory

as old as the printed book
before that
                    "sympathetic history"

that's not what happened

There is no substitute

It must be done here
It must be done now

There is nowhere to go

inconsolable pressure to
emerge

There is no hope of having
anything else

It is only conceivable that you be it

The impulse and instinct will carry you
through,

writing what's uppermost, without delay

which strickens

which strictness

a year of sustained political activity

"But no one can know until she has
reached where

it is not."

I can hear the water in the fountain.

There is water in the fountain now that

it has rained. Now that it has rained

and I must go to work again. The chairs

are bolted down but you can move the table.

We have no poetic. A public house. The dream

of an enormous book. I can't count on you for

anything before Nine. Make it up. An ominous,

enormous book. An onerus anonymous ominous

book that found in the movement of an arm

or leg a proof of life. This is the fading

document thereof.

The world

will not be made into a sophisticated book.

This rough extended way. Shakespeare

is everywhere. Poetry which knows

itself as force. Those who are brought

through Poetry have never found any more

moving, latent, expectant—the most real thing.

The book I have been reading is called

the Angel of the Oppressed. She followed

the Niedergasse out of town toward Lichtenstein

and Zwickern. Violence emanating from the Real.

The 'thing' that is history. "The new age

opened up by the stroke of an ax at Whitehall

on 30 January 1649," Trotsky, *History of*

the Russian Revolution.

["Bare fist relational"
Myung Mi Kim

We only who

who undergo

something unresolved has been deferred

double that of the hard decade, her Eisenhower jacket

What is real and what is not

                              deplete. defeat.

Compelling need for narration

Dissemble the falsehood of my saying to my friend

When you say you are their music

The phenomenon of an unprinted book

a thread of figuration

ferocity of statement

erasures and displacement

A single fields which I have looked upon

That's no different
from slamming the door

"I was out of my mind"

Rites out of a pitiless world, she said with a pitiless
laugh,

Youth are stepping
Youth stepping forward
Youth stepping
forward youth stepping

Raul Gonzalez (Armour plant in Kansas City)

"When the majority of workers are Mexican."

You do the rounds. You go where there's work.

Connie, "airing." Bob, "you are generalizing."

Joe, "But we're doing struck work in our plant."

Trade Union Action League in Birmingham.

You look at the problem
You draft resolutions
You vote, and then you act.

Workers who want to organize among themselves
to better their own situation?

Marginal indication of a desire
that must be suppressed at all cost.

A threat
to cross over from one to the other

to enter the public sphere

Done what harm to whom.

Ten minutes after crossing, the replacement workers
returned and joined the pickets

Shortages
deteriorating
into speeches

The sessions spilled over
into the second shift

The individual, a form of life,
complex, ambiguous, equivocal

reproducing confusion and arrives

our captive Held captive

a twist
on the wrist
upraised
clenched fist

shallow

the shadow

of idea

posited A

and that was

the last we saw

of America

coda

If this

is error

and against

me proved,

I never

wrote,

and no

one ever

loved.

26.IX.81
rime 81

He, who has
government,

who makes my heart
his den,

can shape
no phrase

Sit with grief, who see their friends

There was a time,
a time long ago,

faces frown, or look away

By lonely roads, at night,
seek my house

Wept for,

hand cradled head
like Rose,
grief's capital

swayed in the storm, undid

(what skirt in tatters

he asked her who she was

"Accept,
interspersed, kinship,

am Justice, gave you bread"

Now she had made her
future clear

Hold of my lord,

burn what it would

Beside the pure wave, at my side

This lovely child, the other
sitting,

make it hard for him
to start,

distraught,

unseeing
untaught

and taking up
this gold,
your thought

disuse, and others born

a beggar's bowl

we count the toll

all alone, stone
our house is built

fair goal, white bloom

intensity,

has made
a fault
my son

my song,

make all
your colors
the snowy

not what I am
will keep
ajar

FLYING MACHINE

"the Soul selects
her own Society"

Until upon entering
the open fields get
to the wine & ling

er in an English &
sociable way as if
all the malignity

about the beginning
of October most of
which I will copy

what great change
can arrive worn but
that women are, a

sealed book to me
while beyond what
I thought I was

traversed with speed
& ease & that fine Day
the impossible society

she finds slight re
source in her sister's
house, aerial navigation

experience of the mort
ifications my writing &
my earning money suffer

& be dull & shut
up I cannot stand
the impertinence of

acquaintance dark on
the subject to which
you allude as if you

like to leave it empty
a clog obliged to econo
mize & think on econo

my all day long packed
with wool round stone
for the man at Florence

by Jamaica & Sidney,
Panama, Australia, New
Guinea & here in my

island prison were not
teaching in any way the
worst of all to be tried

& talk of surmises
I have no heart for that
& cling to my child as

my sole tie, ceremony
magnificence, Venice-
Munich returning by

the Rhine is but mere
outline & bare bones
she left me thinking

the sound of Prague
too much to be dwell
ing on the minutia

—the trash—those way
wardnesses about like
the original as a home

resembles a skeleton
give the Bear my moth
er's monograph, the

panic & poverty of
years were any defect
in the drawing indulge

lilac drag mention
the first turning to
the left at the last

iron gate the first
open door every idle
& evil tale give them

to the messenger &
in the prevented pages
of German & Irish poets

of distant date
in print—subject of
—object—or subject—I

else we must be revo
lutionised as if you
leave it empty my sign

manual that he is not
just now forests afford
ing worse than wandering.

"My face is my fortune,
Sir" lead white oil paint
from the nursery rhyme

"Where are you going,
pretty Maid?" also the
Chronicle of the Abbot

of Croyland, some change
some terrible event ex
pected from our northern

miseries it is the
beams & rafters the
Tidings from Field

Place the tower of
flesh whose life
hangs on the beam.

Dear Robert Frost,
the Shanty Irish
kicked you off

the hill the loss
less felt & lamented
it is a thousand pities.

Deplorably, dispirited
she sensible incapable
I took her some jelly,

oranges, sponge cakes
& her favorite kale
for the surface is all

I know this time twelve
months from the hands
of your Clerk & my cap

ital friend Mr. Camden
—first edition—far
advanced in a Romance

legibly & now in Italy
in a land & the author
of the Last Man every

scrap of writing marks
remaining on & make
a sickhouse of it as

before now I did all
my life scant pages
deployed which I have

faithfully transcribed
not exactly as in Virgil
a narrow gold ribbon

round Daedalus never
wound my resource to
return a ray his sub

jects her thoughts as
for the merit of my
adaptation the stone

crop & soap dish must
wait as until I did all
my life would willingly

leave her to her
fate—that wretched
fate—of wife space

is governed as to the
tone to be assumed &
what to say to the day

of no longer insisting
on it let me have the
signed page rendered

timid thru adversity
reading & collecting
at least let it be too

large it is comfortable
& expectant of its guests
—agora—the public place

in spite of the Lord
Chancellor & suspension
act ought we not to be

happy & so we are so
unhappy my little bird
is dragging a broken

wing behind him yet
can you think of any
other I must write

in a hurry & hasten
ing as I wish to be
contemptuous in the

library of his house
the terror I have of
every accident happen

ing there is less con
tention of classes here
than England I must be

more industrious as to
the event you allude to
plumpes denken she said

with scant intellect &
put the honest father
to the refuge whether

in Naples, Rome or Athens
offers us objects we value
highly aggregates encroach

another order—an order
of value—an imperfect
faculty not the subject

ivity that refers to Mr.
Hope you remember Mr.
Hope? It is a policy.

My roots are torn up.
What makes me most
impatient of all is that

tedious, germinating
patience of the ox
pulling the plow

the living page prop, stay
& pioneer man woman
& child & child & child

she said with scant
intellect no end to
the sea between sign

& event the Field of
Sound susceptibility
to influence perfection

of capacity awakening
a mass of fallen five
black olives on a saucer

art building space into
every production I cannot
come to London will you

come to London will you
come to me as soon as
you can my little boy

is very well he is a
very lovely child we
resemble the mob in

this respect also
injunction repulses
all real help my spur

ious solidarity not
strong & for the most
part it is events that

happen round & let
results & prospects
a feather for a sail

to which I have said
with the abject and re
spectful deference of

my class these are the
masterpieces ceaselessly
the scene often leaving

you at Kentish Town the
veil is torn now having
made the effort to begin

to write call David,
Becky, Bob, call Ann
in Iowa City history

we lived off the land
tied to the land 110
day coal strike 7000

out at different plants
a fraction of value. We
have no country China

a nation that shuts
disaster done in the name
up till yet. These

are a few of my favorite things
when the wind blows
when the sky grows

cold in the coalfields
of Appalachia a row of
pictures pencilled cap

illaries Join the Army
Junk some kind of first
intelligence back to

stop at random on the
road we build big & we
lived high on the hog

what happened to those
people one of the many
thousands of my class

a good deal of dust
silk & satin fashioned
fortune every bit of it

effects of English manu
facture my reach & rea
son painted on the page

I have this from a book
she wrote a sort of story
admiring, auditory, I had

the honor & well reward
the reading out of the
goodness roving poring

pudding a sort of sea
port effect reflect ex
actly whether the work

men a company of men
passionate were trying
announcements on the

title page I could never
figure out what that was
for I live indoors a small

house in a quiet way
& studied geography
take me along take

along prohetic Arabia
a copy of D'Alembert
in French I so much

like to hear talk French
London could be with me
our house in America

a library lock & key
a vision of the date
tree summoned French

like land fuzzy stuff
beautiful sailors how
factory & farm boys

would turn back to
look at me as I went
by their language

their way of life
since I loved them
youth has fled

I was waiting a little
breathlessly to break
a corner off & offer

or for us to meet as
equals Kan't concept
the Wrath of the Beau

tiful in Hegel, Galileo
star light, star bright
prayer is my cry tonight

unqualified praise for
the laboring poor the pardon
scene & argument between

the clerk of Zurich
Naboth will cry out
tyrannical lassitudes

endorsed with answers
either shrinking up or
stretching out & not

to be reversed
Hypobololemaioi!
—figures of excess—

let any look over the rolls
peril & we were parted
Eurydice was past invoking

prize & reprizal
around the world that
use the capital "C"

& every one of their
extensions sweet keep
it as my token this

redoubling of the same
affirmation saying two
times the one thing

even ahead of the over
throw honeycomb stone
pendulous excrescencies

this is in every sense
one of the major Eng
lish vernacular manu

scripts this is where
war is actually being
waged only the opening

the new proletariat
the contribution we
bring not as a current

that holds state power
or even influences any
major wing of the labor

movement or national
liberation struggle
in any country today.

Not on a shell she
starts, archaic for
the sea coming up

out of the still recent
but sharply separated
past of our workinggirl

years I was a revolution
ist a superannuated form
though her own subsistance

was precarious & will she
speak that French about
the matter in the interest

of the child we have
taken up the child
to look for lollipops

for a little boy a ballad
with a wood cut on top
a jumping game & panto

mime taken up. What
is not the laws whose
laws you begin to think

socially & act politically
the working class as long
as there is another option

will not look to itself
this is the point where we
decide to pose the possibility

what we are saying & what
we are not saying at the
question of the crossroads.

Steelworkers cut in half in
two years the act of writing
fictive being she lay calling

for from a pallet in the pen
itentiary a logic of need more
fit to guide Martin Luther

King's marvelous new militancy
you are not no longer now
the crowd had again increased

continuing to increase she
laughed & said "I am writing"
she slipped and fell a work

man caught her & she was not
killed pulling away far away
out of sight and into the sea

if necessary she was pushing
away her only child who looked
at her with round astonished

into round astonished eyes.
It is what it is & has the
infinite within it. The women

had no choice but to work
when heavy with child
& many were forced to repair

to a stable or loft to manage
as best they could much as
in Bethlehem threw herself to

the earth long before my guide,
how I met him & where the media
de prendre ou de mettre to take

or to put dans la main d'autrui
in someone else's hand en silence
une piece de monnaie silently

a coin in silence Mallarmé
O.C. page 368. I cannot
go to London an activity

transforming the fact.
Outside is the fact.
Face torn between pity

& a helpless
glance
The face

put too
close to
the form

Red Desert
Out of the
Blue I don't

exist any
more even
that rings

untrue,
address to
the voices

a theater
of voices
malevolent
                    volent

                        they fly or
                            are flying

It was on the
evening of May,
1, 1919, the uproar

we later learned
was Landauer struck
& again struck with

a heavy blow by the
soldier who shouted,
Dog! A shot rang

out as we went thru
the gate as we went
along thru the building

we had to pass back
across & saw the body
who in Germany today

remembers his books
on Shakespeare, Hölderlin,
Whitman? My life

is a miracle of 40 years
not pickt from the leaves
of any author those tatter

ed regiments convuls't
a divided & endless vol
ume that lies expans'd

a publick manuscript
that will one day be
our own case who spy

the signatures & single
out a face. The practice
I cannot manifest no more

than parallel in poets
among the militants
how many wounds

have been given
for the victory
the contempt

of the calling
in those days
scorned & derided

& pointed at
like a bird.
My little bird

is dragging a broken
wing behind her simpled
further such as are not

full without a handful
fit for onely those who lapt
in the winter like dogges

a sort of plebian bone.
Machiavelli's profile
disappointed me tutelary

I would not omit a copy
a classicism often rounded
out this was sometimes

parcel of & the tables
written on both sides.
What counts is always

only the next stop at
any place depicted from
time to time & called the time

& place. Toys & other items
for the child one franc
& the Duc d'Aumaule's

pamphlet against Plon-
Plon bought for a shilling
on Brompton Road.

A reading list jotted
on back of a bar napkin
does that constitute

a contract to teach? How
false how patently false
they wanted to take me to see

CEMENT. Maggie May
my sobriquet proper
poles & epicycles all

my own complexionally
indisposed for community
have hardly even time.

There is no church can
command my obedience
to a canon more confined

to the order & economy
of one body knit loosely
minced into atoms. This

is all the history we will
ever have that I had
wonder what woman

it were. The contingency
of one poet reading another
means if the page doesn't

have it no imagination
on my part as to what
I might read into it

has no significance.
I hope everybody would
read me the same way.

This activity has little
to do with learning.
The thing in form is to

be free in whatever form
is used a free form does
not assure freedom so

that it comes to this:
I believe in freedom
regardless of form.

Supine high strung
once we leave the
lawyer's office

the problem of a
period style emer
gency sally boding

sound deemed off
scourings have hard
ly even time & the

idea never comes
into the mind.
Plurality as

in an allegory
whipped those
out of church

which bought
& sold reformed
the coin grope

after & divided
was but his Art
conjoyne & obscure

each other October
1602. An ironized
term this is cause

for throwing a pair
of dice these are
the masterpieces

eleemosynaries down
beat antics (the paren
thesis on the Party

as large as the main
theme) this frame is
raised upon a mass

impulsive emotional
intensity impovisation
their life work returns

of one series when no
element first or last
who would measure

all objects mercilessly
numerable forms an
instrument of fun

ction continuous co
hesion accomplisment
a practical labor pur

ple or people like an
echo "construction of
proofs in an infinite

series" setting a pur
pose merely caprice
muscular nervous rea

ctions "a rigid con
cept of the calculation
of means" teeming some

one gets pushed up front
to speak/extract/they
hold up a single page

in the air & cry for
joy, Dictatorship
of the Proletariat!

That there might
be a name for it
the strongest ref

erent my experience
not pity for the poor
"these half steps"

James (Mac) Warren
National Secretary
Socialist Workers

Party "these baby
steps" we are in a
war of attrition how

far can the local go
if the local has the will?
There is no foolproof way

"the Brother here hit it"
(you will have to fight)
tactics linkages greetings

grievances a range they
lock you out USX, Phelps-
Dodge, PATCO, P-9 our story

[a note of excessive caution]
the fight against the indict
ment of the 18 "the necessary

abuse that comes with every
struggle worth something"
our story "I am not a public

speaker" this is what happened
in Austin a meeting took place
in a park women with flashlights

"some of us went to jail that day
& it was the best day of our life"
a flash of what she said what we

know what she said in honor of
our German American ancestry
people under the heel a fun

night of Christian music
Randalia! laughter she
will carry with her always

& it is radical. Me too.
I was born. I want to live.
Our story that UFCW bastard

a buddy of Mitch's threatening
the town at a mass meeting
a town that did not want

the new IBP plant & the farmers
articulate about the damage
—the toll—& that class

collaborationist union bum
threatened them all with an
invasion of Mexicans/Asians

head on/competition the system
we are chained in. The tele
phone, a ringing object.

Who's there? The Creditor.
To state the matter briefly
I hope to reach you before

you reach me I hope that
by reaching you to initiate
conditions the State is not

a theoretical concept
& politics are real are
unassimilable in the elec

toral mode rethink in light
of everything new that has
occurred proclaim for the

West the left in the West
& this is no more than the
need to found theoretical

stanzas schöner Schein

                    spoon
               the Ponds

Lukács: "strong, simple
blonds striding confidently
along" White Guards in the

widest sense the refusal
of science I do not share
it/biology/otherwise all you

are the book any book bound
by it. Shadow of prison
aware of a shadow attached

to his shadow anticipate
so as to live thru an in
mate. 25 years. The police

of that city hit system
upstairs punishment of
a purely physical kind

despite all this pain he
raised his head from time
to time this is a fact.

The many roads...
"I have my flowers
outside in the sun"

Mandelstam wound up
on the dump to even
enunciate it is to be

thrown into an
entirely private
articulation.

I enclose with this
your sketch 'Execution'
but I must ask you to

give me a declaration
in writing that you
will not try to publish

the sketch while in prison
Zum Personalakt Nieder
schönenfeld 3 Sept. 1920.

Dear Mary, I have never
belonged to any 'school'
what seems range to you

is the new disgust
with language common
to the many poets

in my time. I have
believed in the power
of Socialism, that,

perhaps, was my life's
lie perhaps, Socialism?
Friar Fake & Friar Fuck

always remembering how
personal women always
are I'm ready to give

them up the minute
it will help the cause.
I mean London. Real

London. The London mob.
Arid-looking Arab French
such as you dream by in

Froissart indefatigable
delight foliage portfolios
alongside the spankerboom

polyrhythmic multispatial
streamings of their fever
flag from the steerage

while at sea the Bride
presently cried O, God,
I, Sir! But all this is

philosophy there is no
delirium to conceive our
selves urinals or whence

Lucan learned to say it
is the method of Charity
to suffer into verities

there is no road or ready
way runnes counter to the
multitude the practice

knowledg/the riddle of the
Fishermen for a comment
see Pseudodoxia Ep' one

common philosophy I learned
in the schools the revolution
ary passion obscurity of origin

& condition in the Oneiro
critical Verses of Astram
psychus & Nicephorus done

by none wits more ripe
accept my rhyme he made
a law & them in awe

mirror error claspings
of Wake a mark lament
able remainder destitute

of honor talk cheap as
tape/baton tress taper
garner garment/worker.

In reply, infringed omni
science the soul of all that
was excluded or imagined

as another had revealed
it this is consolation con
tinual comfort & security.

This was a bold & open
accusation the mention of
her name made me start

& tremble the endless
indecision concerning
her an agony better far

better to avoid her nor
address her often as she
passed whole hours walking

up & down the daughter
of her thought formed
of bark rich with works

to read & rally
the scattered causes
that live to ransom

truth Nature twists
when near the Sun
to the Abyss there

will I sit with souls
like stars my mind
diseased disease

my luckless frame
work I no whit reck
but feed on shadows

whiles I die for food.
Mac: "lies, all lies,
ignorance, stupidity,

falsehood." Zuk:
"truth requires
proof of love."

Not yet capable
no longer not yet
what strange ruins

went to school.
Book, I would buy
you t'instruct me

gainst such heart
pierc'd demonstration
& warme it to pity

that the contending
kingdoms thrust in
between the factions

swear against those
whose proof is not Fancy
wants (its noun) wants

(its unit) from the stomach
or from Fancy I was walking
in a good man's shop whose

head was crowned with thorns
whose face was spit on & body
broken La Vigne's discussion

about the composing of his work
dar non harm don hym ne may me
venge a drawing of a man a layer

of matter & drawing fend betray
entail pent abhor countless
kindnesses "I am the Night

arrived late from abroad"
between her & me there is
a secret sympathy read to

ruin sounding in the ears day
& night no hap can greater
hazard bring as casual of

disaster he doe use which he
had held but the space of 9
months & 4 days the Justice

of the cause "to us a child
is born to us a Son is given
& the government shall be

upon his shoulders & her name
shall be called Wonderful."
Isaiah. 9.6. Al was Medea

Sche what him best thoghte
Sche thoghte how sche was
deceived Sche unmete he

thoghte to restore & felle
& thoughte if that he seide
it oute lustes fonde thurgh

the fendes prively to fonde
ayein Rome to rebelle that
other held him stille hire

thoughte a thousand year
as their deserved. A poet
who had sprung from the lord

knows where & had such bad
teeth. Proust: "Flaubert? No
metaphor." Magee? A riot

of autonomy—civics incarnate—
what is accomplished by writing
someone else's book they could

not get a reading on my right
eye falling away & the scales
peel the rocks the roots the

pavement cornices mortar
crust curves these corners
those walls a rural memory

has fused into a city
the Roman villa was a
prison pure. We raise

the question Marc Bloch
asked on the eve of his
murder by the Nazis in

that case worth five &
a half oxen or five hogs
the Taurian goddess deity

of Slaughter what was needed
was the heart that would make
it impossible. Christianity is

a slave's religion, Marxism
is a slave's indigestion coarse
woolen cloak for the commoner

a vocabulary graceless antinomian
ism dissonance impression
though we may not call them

by the name expound Humanity
commonwealth verbatim endorsed
with answers & saw that the case

was each of ours as in your
eyes I am nothing & the price
everything the last hour

doch noch "my success"
she said "is that we
are not dead" her words

I remember them exactly
some Dakota City people
have visited that's about all

have them send a dozen more
Bud Schulte/Killfloor Steward
"this cannot be just another

social event" the answer
is not evident. How does
Emma G. define ice in an

oily rag? Jammed dome
obtrude far from home
or the farm or factory

those who allocate public
funds aim for despair
ethical questions we are

just now beginning to ask
first a few words about
Europe forced to look on

fatalistically as events fly
by Native Land Dwindle
the fragility of naming

& experience of its negation
as undergone by a generation
of poets at the outskirts

of the State has brought
English Poetry to the task
of confronting the last

I had never seen except
in a dream & tried hard not
to count heavy paragraphs

made of wax I made up their
names like water, like glass
all the while with an ear

to the real the burning wheel
to prove him herself to him
if I had my own face again

as for her face the waste
her day kept warm
jets of steam that

rose thru the zinc
on which they lay
chanting tactics a

few people filter
in hadn't we better
not keep quiet?

May 2, 1985
Before 10:00 a.m.
University of Iowa.
President's door.
Youth are chanting
Free Mandela!

December 18, 1994
3:00 - 6:00 a.m.
The Witch's Hour.
Big Lagoon, Humbolt.
"Once, on the Pac
ific," Rbt. Frost